SQL/400

by Example

James Coolbaugh

®
A Division of
DUKE COMMUNICATIONS INTERNATIONAL

221 E. 29th Street • Loveland, CO 80538
(800) 621-1544 • (970) 663-4700 • www.29thStreetPress.com

Library of Congress Cataloging-in-Publication Data

Coolbaugh, James, 1961-
   SQL/400 by example / by James Coolbaugh.
   p. cm.
   Includes index.
   ISBN 1-58304-030-7 (pbk.)
   1. IBM AS/400 (Computer)—Programming. 2. SQL (Computer program
language) I. Title.
   QA76.8.I25919 C675 1999
   005.75'65—dc21
                                              98-58126
                                              CIP

 ® Published by 29th Street Press®
DUKE COMMUNICATIONS INTERNATIONAL
Loveland, Colorado

© 1999 by James Coolbaugh

This book was printed and bound in Canada.

ISBN 1-58304-030-7

2002 2001 2000 WL 2 1 10 9 8 7 6 5 4 3

This book is dedicated to my wife Pam
and my children Michael and Hannah.

Their love, support, and especially their patience
have made this book possible.

Table of Contents at a Glance

Table of Contents

Chapter 1

What Is SQL?

SQL stands for Structured Query Language. SQL was developed at IBM labs in the 1970s with the idea of providing an English-like language with which to access a database. But SQL is more than just a query language; SQL lets you create database files and make changes to a database file.

Standard SQL statements can run on many different operating systems. Therefore, once you have mastered SQL on one machine, you can use it on any other machine that has SQL. However, SQL is not a magic tool. You still must have an excellent understanding of your database to effectively extract the data you need. Without that knowledge, SQL won't help you any more than any other query tool will.

On the AS/400, SQL is part of the base operating system. However, unless you purchase a third-party package or SQL/400, you cannot easily execute SQL statements. This book focuses on both the SQL/400 product offered by IBM and the other SQL statements available.

The SQL offered on the AS/400 contains many of the same functions as SQL offered on other platforms. However, IBM has incorporated some new functions not available on other platforms. Likewise, some SQL functions available on other platforms may not be available on the AS/400. We make no attempt in this book to compare SQL on the AS/400 to other SQL products available.

Before we discuss the available SQL statements, let's look at several of the components of SQL and the features available with the SQL/400 product.

SQL LANGUAGE COMPONENTS

We can break the SQL language into four basic types of statements: Data Definition Language (DDL), Data Manipulation Language (DML), Dynamic SQL, and miscellaneous. Two of these components — DDL and DML — are called languages to differentiate their purpose from that of other SQL statements, but both are part of SQL.

Data Definition Language (DDL)

DDL consists of those statements that let you create, delete, and control access to SQL libraries, files, indexes, views, and packages. These statements are similar to the CRT (create), DLT (delete), GRT (grant), and RVK (revoke) commands on the AS/400.

Data Manipulation Language (DML)

DML consists of those statements that let you read, update, add, and delete records in a database file. DML statements are the ones you will use most often.

Also included in this category are those statements used during the programming of SQL statements in a high-level language (HLL), such as RPG or Cobol.

Dynamic SQL Statements

Dynamic SQL statements are those statements that require SQL to interpret and execute at the time they are encountered in an HLL program. These statements require greater overhead when they are processed in an HLL program.

Miscellaneous Statements

Miscellaneous statements include all statements that do not fall into the above three categories. As with any language, you will use the various types of SQL statements as you need them. You need to remember that, with a few exceptions, you can use almost any statement at any time. The main exceptions are those statements that are used solely within an HLL program.

SQL/400 PRODUCT FEATURES

The SQL/400 product consists of several different features that offer you a variety of methods for entering and executing SQL statements. We cover each of these components in more depth later in this book.

Interactive SQL

Interactive SQL performs exactly as its name implies. With Interactive SQL, you can enter, prompt, and execute any nonprogramming SQL statement interactively. The benefit of this component is that you can enter and execute SQL statements quickly — particularly useful when you want to run ad hoc queries or process an SQL statement you are not likely to be using multiple times.

SQL/400 Query Manager

SQL/400 Query Manager is a function similar to the Program Development Manager (PDM). This feature lets you enter and save SQL statements that you may want to execute on a more permanent basis. You can execute saved SQL statements at any time and in any environment (for example, from within a CL program). SQL/400 Query Manager also provides better report formatting capabilities than those available with Interactive SQL.

Embedded SQL

Embedded SQL offers the capability to embed SQL statements in an HLL program, such as RPG or Cobol, and to execute those statements in a controlled environment. Programming SQL within an HLL program is more involved and takes longer to learn than other SQL topics. However, you will want to learn this part of SQL because it will give you yet another tool for writing better systems and programs.

SQL/400 Terminology

Many of the terms used with SQL differ from those with which an AS/400 programmer generally is familiar. However, each term translates easily into concepts familiar to AS/400 programmers. We explain some of the main SQL terms here; for clarity, we use AS/400 terms wherever appropriate. The following are some of the basic terms you'll encounter when you use SQL, and what they mean.

Alias — An alias is a special name used to reference a table or view. An alias is a special Distributed Data Management (DDM) type of file that is created within the collection. With aliases you can specify the member name for a table.

Application server — This term refers to the environment or location that is executing the SQL application. In other words, the application server identifies the relational database to which you are currently connected, either the local machine or a remote database on a network.

Binding — Binding is the process of linking a program's SQL statements with the database. The SQL precompiler builds a definition of the statements to be executed and the optimum access method for each SQL statement. Binding allows for faster execution of the SQL statements within a program.

Clause — A clause is a portion of an SQL statement that lets you perform a specific operation within that statement. A clause is analogous to parameters on a command. Each clause lets you specify how a statement is to be processed.

Collection — A collection is a repository for all objects created by SQL. A collection is the same as a library. In fact, when you create a collection, the object type is *LIB.

Column — A column is an individual data element within a row. A column is the same as a field.

Column function — A column function performs a summary type operation over a group of records. The result of a column function is a single value. A column function is equivalent to a group summary operation or to level break totals.

Correlated name — A correlated name is an alias that lets you qualify data in an SQL statement. Using a correlated name lets you quickly qualify fields with the same name in different files. This also is the method used to pass data to a subselect.

Cursor — A cursor is a pointer used by embedded SQL statements to move through a table. A cursor identifies the currently active record.

Index — An index is a definition of how to sort a table. An index is the same as a logical file. When you create an index, the object type is *LF.

Predicate — A predicate refers to a set of comparison operations for determining whether some task is to be performed, such as to say, "If the following conditions are true, perform the task." A predicate can be a simple test or it can involve more complicated logic. SQL provides several special comparison functions that allow for more powerful relationship testing than normally is available.

Resulting table — A resulting table is the final list of fields and records extracted from the files specified on a SELECT statement. We use this term throughout the book.

Row — A row is a single set of columns within a table. A row is the same as a record.

SQL package — An SQL package is an object that contains control information required to execute a distributed SQL application.

Table — A table is a definition of the columns that make up a row. A table is the same as a physical file. When you create a table, the object type is *PF.

Token — A token is an SQL term that refers to the valid keywords and operators for each SQL statement. If you type something wrong, you will receive a message that an invalid token was encountered. Simply put, the syntax of the statement is incorrect.

View — A view is a predefined access method for retrieving rows from a table. A view is a special object that links a logical file and an SQL SELECT statement together.

SQL SYNTAX

When working with SQL statements, you must follow certain rules and methods of entry regardless of the statement you are entering or where you are entering it. In this section, we provide some of these rules and also help you get a feel for how SQL statements look. We make no attempt here to explain the meanings of the statements shown.

Statement Entry

When examples are shown in most SQL books and manuals, the statements are presented in such a way that you can easily identify each part of the statement. The typical approach is to enter all clauses and keywords in capital letters, to show each clause of the statement on separate lines, and to indent the statement. While these criteria usually help you understand the statement, they are not necessary for the statement to execute.

You can enter SQL statements and clauses in lowercase or capital letters, and you can enter them on the same line or on consecutive lines. The only requirement is that you separate clauses and keywords by at least one space.

It is recommended, however, that you enter SQL statements in a way that someone else can quickly understand what you are trying to accomplish. This is especially true when you are embedding SQL statements in an HLL program or when you are using SQL/400 Query Manager. Even when you are using interactive SQL, it is best to follow this approach until you are comfortable with each SQL statement.

For example, the following statements are valid, regardless of how they are entered:

```
1. SELECT CUST#, NAME
      FROM CUSTMAST
     WHERE STATE = 'CA'

   SELECT CUST#, NAME FROM CUSTMAST WHERE STATE = 'CA'

   select cust#, name from custmast where state='CA'

2. CREATE TABLE PRODLIB/CATEGORY
      (CTGRY#      DEC(3,0 )  NOT NULL WITH DEFAULT,
       CTDESC      CHAR(25)   NOT NULL WITH DEFAULT)

   CREATE TABLE PRODLIB/CATEGORY (CTGRY# DEC(3,0) NOT NULL WITH
   DEFAULT,CTDESC CHAR(25) NOT NULL WITH DEFAULT)

   create table prodlib/category (ctgry# dec(3,0) not null with
   default,ctdesc char(25) not null with default)

3. DELETE FROM SALESHST
     WHERE SHPDTE<920101
       AND CUST#=1583

   DELETE FROM SALESHST WHERE SHPDTE<920101 AND CUST#=1583

   delete from saleshst where shpdte<920101 and cust#=1583
```

As you can see from these examples, statements are easier to understand when they are entered on separate lines and indented. This principle is especially true when you start to enter larger and more complex SQL statements.

At times, a list of values is entered in part of an SQL clause or built-in function. When you specify the list, you must separate each element in that list by a comma. You are not required to provide any spaces between the values, but you must include the commas.

File Processing

When you are working with file names in any SQL statement, you must keep several things in mind:

- If you want to qualify what library a file is in, you do so by using the same syntax as you would for referencing any other place on the AS/400 (i.e., Library/File). The exception to this rule is that if you have specified the use of SAA definitions instead of native AS/400 definitions, you would use a period (.) instead of a slash (/). If you do not specify a library, your current library list will be searched for the first file with that name.

- The type of file you specify can be any valid physical or logical file on the system, with a few exceptions. Whether the file was created with DDS, IDDU, SQL, or some other method, you can more than likely process the file in SQL. Even files with no external field definition can be processed, but there are limits to what you can perform. In other words, SQL does not require that the file being processed be created by SQL. This is a very important point, because it means you can execute SQL statements over your existing database files.

- You cannot process a file that has more than one record format. There is no mechanism in SQL to tell the computer to use a specific format. Therefore, multiple-format logical files are not allowed.

- If a file has more than one member, the *FIRST (first created) member is processed. There are two methods for specifying a specific member for processing within an SQL statement. The first is by using the OVRDBF command to point to the member. The second is by means of an alias. An alias is a defined name within SQL that points to a file and optionally to a specific member. (See Chapter 8 for more information about aliases.)

- Also, when using the OVRDBF command, you can specify the library that is to be used. If you specify the library on the OVRDBF command, that library will be used, even if you qualify the file name on the SQL statement. As long as the override is in effect, that library will be used for that file.

Data Fields

When you are working with data fields and using them in computational operations, the basic rules discussed below apply to each type of field.

NUMERIC VALUES

You can perform arithmetic operations against numeric values at almost any time. The valid numeric operations are addition (+), subtraction (-), multiplication (*), division (/), and exponentiation (**). These are the only math operators that are allowed. More complicated math functions are handled with built-in functions.

Also, for the most part, you can use different types of numeric values together, such as a packed decimal field and a floating-point field. You will need to be careful with such combinations, especially when you are working with floating-point values: Errors might occur because of the varying degrees of precision available to different data types on the AS/400.

CHARACTER VALUES

When you are working with character values, no single character value can exceed 32,766 characters. When you specify a string value, the value must be enclosed with apostrophes (') — you cannot use a quotation mark ("). The exception to this rule is for Cobol, where you can change the default string identifier and use quotation marks instead of apostrophes. This exception is true only when you specify Cobol for the SQL environment.

The last thing to keep in mind regarding character values is that they are case-sensitive. This means that capital and lowercase letters are distinct from one another and will affect comparisons and sorting.

The only operator allowed for character values is the concatenation (| |) operator. Functions such as *BCAT and *TCAT, with which many AS/400 programmers are familiar, are not available, although some built-in functions, when used with the concatenation (| |) operator, will create the effect of *BCAT or *TCAT. In addition to using the | | symbol for concatenation, you can use the special operator CONCAT. In fact, it is recommended that you use the special operator CONCAT instead of the | | symbol because the | | symbol is not part of the SQL standard and the | character may not be the same on another non-AS/400 computer.

DATE VALUES

Three different types of date values are available on the AS/400: DATE, TIME, and TIMESTAMP. We use the term *date value* to mean any of these three types. We indicate when a function or task is specific to a given type.

The only valid arithmetic operators allowed with date fields are those of addition (+) and subtraction (-). At times, you can work with character string values that represent a date format. When you do this, you must ensure that you follow the rules for the date; you also may be required to use one of the built-in functions for handling dates.

The operands for date arithmetic will consist of date values and/or numeric values. The numeric operands are referred to as *durations*. The result of data arithmetic is either a date value or a duration.

NULL VALUES

You must be careful when you perform calculations with null-capable fields (fields that can contain null values). For example, whenever you perform any type of arithmetic operation or concatenation on a field within a record where the value of that field is null, the result is a null value. However, when you perform summary operations, null values are normally ignored.

Chapter 2

Data Manipulation Language

SQL's data manipulation language is a very powerful tool for accessing a database. With SQL, you can access files created by SQL, DDS, or IDDU. To a limited degree, you also can process files with no external file definition.

The statements we discuss here are those statements that let you read/list (SELECT), update (UPDATE), add (INSERT), and delete (DELETE) records in a file.

In this chapter, we explain the basic concepts of each statement. We will explain the more complicated and involved tasks in the following chapters, along with data examples. That way, you can work on one concept, master it, then move on.

THE SELECT STATEMENT

The purpose of the SELECT statement is to extract records from a file and present those records either to your screen, a printer, a database file, or an HLL program. The SELECT statement is the equivalent of a QUERY list or an HLL read statement. You will probably find the SELECT statement to be one of the most useful statements because you can use it to perform many complicated operations against a file.

The basic premise behind the SELECT statement is simple. You select fields from files where certain conditions are true, or as SQL puts it,

```
SELECT  field(s)
FROM    file(s)
WHERE   condition(s) are true
```

Although the SELECT statement's construct is simple, you are not limited to providing simple list operations. With the SELECT statement you also can

- specify which fields are to be presented

- extract or build your own fields

- join files together

- condition how records are selected

- perform group summary operations

- sort the results in any manner

- combine the results of multiple SELECT statements

- nest SELECT statements within each other

Each of these functions is controlled by a specific clause. Because the clauses are not necessarily dependent on each other, we will give you the full explanation and rules for each clause as we present it. Also, to use some of the clauses, you need to have an understanding of the more complex functions that are available.

The syntax of the SELECT statement is as follows:

```
SELECT [DISTINCT | ALL]
       {* | {{field name | expression [AS column name]},...}}
FROM <library/>file [AS] [alias],...
[WHERE predicate]
[GROUP BY field name,...]
[HAVING predicate]
[UNION [ALL]]
[ORDER BY {field name | relative fld position} [ASC |
DESC],...]
[OPTIMIZE FOR integer [ROW | ROWS]]
[WITH [[NC | NONE] | [UR | CHG] | [RS | ALL] | CS | RR]]
```

The clauses above are listed in the order in which they can be used. You are not required to use any of these clauses, except SELECT and FROM. If you do use any of them, however, they must be in the order listed.

When you are programming the SELECT statement in an HLL program, some additional clauses and keywords are provided. We discuss these in the programming sections of this book. For now, let's discuss how to select specific fields for a given query and how to sort the results.

The SELECT Clause

The purpose of the SELECT clause is to specify the fields that are to be presented in the resulting table. The field to be presented can be a database field, a calculated value, or a literal. You can use any combination of fields. Use a comma to separate all fields in a SELECT clause.

You specify which database fields are to be presented by typing the names of the fields. If you want to list every field in a file, you do so by using an asterisk (*) instead of the field names. This symbol tells the statement to list every field available. When you use the * to list all fields, however, you cannot specify any other fields. Also note that because the field names you use come from the file specified in the FROM clause, the SELECT and FROM clauses work hand in hand.

The total number of fields allowed is 8,000. The total length of all fields selected cannot exceed 32,766 characters.

Whenever you select a field, the default column headings will be extracted from the database file, if column headings are available. If column headings are not available, the name of the field will be used.

Calculated fields, however, will not have meaningful column headings because SQL doesn't know what to use. With the AS subclause, you can redefine the name of any field in the SELECT clause. This column name will be used for the column headings. In addition, you can use this "new" column name in the ORDER BY clause. Renaming a field does not prevent you from using the original field name. The AS subclause is most useful on calculated results.

You place the AS subclause immediately after the field name or calculated expression, but before the comma separating the fields. The column name you enter must be entered between quotation marks (") if there are any blanks in the new column name.

The SELECT clause also gives you the capability to drop duplicate records from the resulting table. You do this by specifying the DISTINCT keyword on the SELECT clause. This is the same concept as specifying UNIQUE on a file created by DDS, with one difference. When you specify UNIQUE in DDS, only the key fields are required to be unique; when you specify DISTINCT, all the selected fields are evaluated to determine duplicate records.

If you specify DISTINCT, the resulting table will be sorted in the order of the fields in this clause, unless you use the ORDER BY clause to override the default.

The FROM Clause

Now that you have specified which fields are to be presented in the resulting table, you must tell SQL where to find those fields. You use the FROM clause to specify the name of the file from which the resulting table is derived. Specifying the fields first, then the file, may seem backward, but this how SQL works. The FROM clause does not specify which records are selected; this is done via the WHERE clause. The FROM clause only identifies which file is being used for this SELECT.

The following examples should give you a general idea of how to select fields from a database file. You can find the files used in these and other examples throughout the book in Appendix A.

1. Let's say you want to list every field for every record in the catalog master file. You can accomplish this with the following statement:

```
SELECT *
  FROM CATALOG
```

2. If you want to list only the catalog number and its description, you can issue this statement:

```
SELECT CATLG#,CATDSC
  FROM CATALOG
```

3. If you want to list, from the catalog master file, every catalog number and the total sales for last year and the current year combined, you can issue a statement like this:

```
SELECT CATLG#, CURYR$+YR1$ AS "Total Sales"
  FROM CATALOG
```

However, this statement

```
SELECT *, CURYR$+YR1$ AS "Total Sales"
  FROM CATALOG
```

is invalid because the * is present simultaneously with additional fields.

4. Now let's say you want to execute the same statement as above, but you would like to include a constant of 'Total Sales:' for every record listed. Notice that this is different from specifying column headings. You can enter the statement as follows:

```
SELECT CATLG#, 'Total Sales:',CURYR$+YR1$
  FROM CATALOG
```

5. If you need to know every unique combination of a customer number and a catalog number in the sales history file, you can issue the following:

```
SELECT DISTINCT CUST#, CATLG#
  FROM SALESHST
```

In each of the cases above, the entire file will be processed and every record will be listed. We discuss specifying conditions for how records are selected in the next chapter.

The ORDER BY Clause

The purpose of the ORDER BY clause is to specify how the resulting table will be sorted. The format of the ORDER BY clause is as follows:

```
ORDER BY {field name | relative position} [ASC | DESC],...
```

The fields specified in the ORDER BY clause must exist in the SELECT clause. You have the option to sort by the field name or by its relative position in the SELECT clause. The capability to specify a field's relative position exists only in the ORDER BY clause. If the field you want to sort is a derived or calculated value, you must use that field's relative position (column number). Again, you must separate the fields with commas. You must remember that the ORDER BY clause is the last clause you specify in the SELECT statement. A final point about the ORDER BY clause is that null values are treated as high values.

The sort default for all fields is ascending sequence. If you want to specify descending sequence, you need to place the keyword DESC after the field name, separated by a space. You also can use the ASC keyword to specify ascending sequence.

The total length of the sorted fields cannot exceed 10,000 characters, and the number of fields sorted cannot exceed 10,000.

If you do not specify the ORDER BY clause, the results may or may not be sorted, depending on what else is specified in the SELECT clause. For example, if the DISTINCT keyword is used in the SELECT clause, the records will be sorted by the order of the fields in the clause.

Generally, however, if you want a sorted list, you should use the ORDER BY clause to ensure the proper results.

The following examples show you a variety of combinations that are allowed with the ORDER BY clause. We have included the actual results of the SQL statements to help clarify the effect of the ORDER BY clause. We also demonstrate how the DISTINCT keyword affects sorting.

1. If you want to produce a listing of all the catalog numbers and their categories in the catalog master file, but you want the list to be in category order, you can issue any of the following statements:

```
SELECT CTGRY#,CATLG#
  FROM CATALOG
 ORDER BY CTGRY#,CATLG#

SELECT CTGRY#,CATLG#
  FROM CATALOG
 ORDER BY CTGRY#,2

SELECT CTGRY#,CATLG#
  FROM CATALOG
 ORDER BY 1,2
```

The above statements produce the results in Table 2.1.

TABLE 2.1
Results of the Select Statements in Example 1

CTGRY#	CATLG#
15	A597-3996A
15	A658-4077A
15	B156-3780A
24	A225-8037A
24	D362-7997A
38	B115-3170A
64	B501-1218D
64	C689-1192D
156	C871-1139C
156	D805-0271C
348	A483-7921B
348	B489-7920B

2. Now assume you want the same list, but you want the catalog numbers to be in descending order within each category. To accomplish this, you can issue any of these statements:

```
SELECT CTGRY#,CATLG#
FROM CATALOG
 ORDER BY CTGRY#,CATLG# DESC

SELECT CTGRY#,CATLG#
  FROM CATALOG
 ORDER BY 1,2 DESC

SELECT CTGRY#,CATLG#
  FROM CATALOG
 ORDER BY 1 ASC, CATLG# DESC
```

These statements produce the results in Table 2.2.

TABLE 2.2
Results of the Select Statements in Example 2

CTGRY#	CATLG#
15	B156-3780A
15	A658-4077A
15	A597-3996A
24	D362-7997A
24	A225-8037A
38	B115-3170A
64	C689-1192D
64	B501-1218D
156	D805-0271C
156	C871-1139C
348	B489-7920B
348	A483-7921B

3. Now let's say you would like to produce a listing of each catalog number in the catalog master file, in descending order, by the combined sales for the current year and last year. To do this, you can enter this statement:

```
SELECT CATLG#, CURYR$+YR1$ AS "Total Sales"
  FROM CATALOG
 ORDER BY 2 DESC, CATLG# ASC
```

This statement produces the results in Table 2.3.

TABLE 2.3
Results of the Select Statement in Example 3

CATLG#	TOTAL SALES
A225-8037A	30030.00
A658-4077A	13487.85
C689-1192D	10208.00
B501-1218D	9420.00
B156-3780A	7413.40
C871-1139C	5119.87
B489-7920B	4516.70
A483-7921B	3629.35
D805-0271C	3319.94
B115-3170A	2925.00
D362-7997A	270.00
A597-3996A	115.98

In this example, you must use the computed field's relative position to sort on that field. You can see from this example that the order of the sorted fields does not have to follow the order of the fields in the SELECT clause.

4. The following example shows how the DISTINCT keyword and ORDER BY clause are used in connection with one another. Assume you want to produce a listing of each unique occurrence of the customer and catalog numbers in the sales history file. You can issue the following statement:

```
SELECT DISTINCT CUST#, CATLG#
FROM SALESHST
```

This statement produces the results in Table 2.4.

TABLE 2.4
Results of the Select Statement in Example 4

CUST#	CATLG#
392	A225-8037A
392	B115-3170A
392	C871-1139C
392	D805-0271C
411	A225-8037A
411	B115-3170A
411	B156-3780A
411	C871-1139C

continued

TABLE **2.4** CONTINUED

CUST#	CATLG#
411	D805-0271C
1583	A483-7921B
1583	B489-7920B
8395	B115-3170A
8395	C689-1192D
8395	D362-7997A
8395	D805-0271C
32418	A597-3996A
32418	A658-4077A
32418	B156-3780A
62990	B501-1218D
62990	C689-1192D

This table is sorted by the customer number, then the catalog number. But let's say you need to have the table sorted by catalog number, then customer number. First, you can switch the order of the fields on the SELECT clause; this will change the sort. However, if you need the fields selected as they are, you can use the ORDER BY clause to change the final sort. The following shows how you would enter this statement:

```
SELECT DISTINCT CUST#, CATLG#
FROM SALESHST
ORDER BY 2, 1
```

This statement produces the results in Table 2.5.

TABLE **2.5**

Results of the Second Select Statement in Example 4

CUST#	CATLG#
392	A225-8037A
411	A225-8037A
1583	A483-7921B
32418	A597-3996A
32418	A658-4077A
392	B115-3170A
411	B115-3170A
8395	B115-3170A
411	B156-3780A
32418	B156-3780A

continued

TABLE **2.5** CONTINUED

CUST#	CATLG#
1583	B489-7920B
62990	B501-1218D
8395	C689-1192D
62990	C689-1192D
392	C871-1139C
411	C871-1139C
8395	D362-7997A
392	D805-0271C
411	D805-0271C
8395	D805-0271C

The OPTIMIZE FOR Clause

The purpose of the OPTIMIZE FOR clause is to improve the performance for some SQL selects. SQL uses different processing methods, depending on the type of selection being made. The OPTIMIZE FOR clause instructs the SQL optimizer to choose the most efficient method for returning records based on the number of rows indicated. This clause is especially useful for interactive queries.

The format of the OPTIMIZE FOR clause is

```
OPTIMIZE FOR integer [ROW | ROWS]
```

The WITH Clause

The purpose of the WITH clause is to specify the isolation level to be used for a statement. We discuss this concept in Chapter 11.

THE UPDATE STATEMENT

The UPDATE statement provides you with the capability to update information in a database file. You may need to change information in a file, but often the records to be updated are either too many to be updated by hand or the conditions that must be met are fairly complex. The UPDATE statement can help you in such situations.

You can use the UPDATE statement to change the values of fields for a given file. When you use the UPDATE statement, you cannot update more than one file at a time. This means that a join operation is not valid. Simply put, the UPDATE statement will only let you change fields in a single file with either a set value, or a calculated value from information in the same record, or from a single value returned from a subselect, which we discuss in Chapter 7. For our understanding here, you need to know that starting with V4R3, you can update a field with information from another file. If you are using an earlier version or release of the operating system, you cannot do this. However, you can update a file with information from other sources with an HLL program. We cover this in Chapters 10 and 11.

You can also update all columns in a row with a subselect. In this case, the subselect specifies a value for every column in the row; the number of columns and the data types must be compatible.

The syntax for the UPDATE statement is as follows:

```
UPDATE <library/>file [AS] [alias]
  SET [field name = (expression | NULL | DEFAULT | subselect) |
        ROW = subselect] ,...
[WHERE predicate]
[WITH [[NC | NONE] | [UR | CHG] | [RS | ALL] | CS | RR]]
```

Note that the WHERE and WITH clauses are optional for the UPDATE statement.

The UPDATE Clause

The UPDATE clause specifies the name of the file that is to be updated. You can specify only one file name. As with the SELECT statement, you can specify an alias for the file name; doing so is useful only when you are using subselects, which we discuss in Chapter 7.

The SET Clause

The SET clause specifies which fields are going to be updated and with what values. You can update a field with a calculated value, with a set value, with a null value if the field is null capable, or with the default value specified for the field. The calculated value must come from information in the same record. Again, each field to be updated must be separated by a comma.

If you specify a single field name in the SET clause and you also specify a subselect, the subselect that is executed must return a single column and a single row.

If you specify the ROW subclause, you must specify a subselect. In this case, the subselect must return a value for every column in the table. The result of the subselect must be a single row.

The WHERE Clause

The WHERE clause specifies which records will be updated. If you do not specify the WHERE clause, all records in the file will be updated. We discuss record selection in the next chapter.

The following examples should give you a general idea of the UPDATE statement's capabilities:

1. Let's say you want to set the current year sales field in the catalog master file to 0. To do so, issue the following statement:

```
UPDATE CATALOG
   SET CURYR$ = 0
```

2. If you want to shift each year's sales figure in the catalog master file into the next year and also set the current year's sales to 0, you can issue the following statement:

```
UPDATE CATALOG
   SET YR2$ = YR1$,
   YR1$ = CURYR$,
   CURYR$ = 0
```

3. Now let's say you want to set the future price field in the catalog master file to the current price plus 10 percent. To do so, you can issue this statement:

```
UPDATE CATALOG
   SET FPRICE = CPRICE  *  1.10
```

THE INSERT STATEMENT

SQL also provides the capability for you to add records to a database file. You do this with the INSERT statement. Often, you might want to add a single record to a file or maybe create an image of a file, selecting only those records that meet some criteria. You can use the INSERT statement to perform these tasks.

There are two methods for inserting data into a file using the INSERT statement: inserting one record at a time and inserting multiple records with a SELECT statement. You also can specify which fields are to be loaded with values and which are to be set with default values.

The syntax for the INSERT statement is as follows:

```
INSERT INTO <library/>file[(field name,...)]
{VALUES (value | NULL | DEFAULT,...) | SELECT statement}
[WITH [[NC | NONE] | [UR | CHG] | [RS | ALL] | CS | RR]]
```

You must use either the VALUES clause or the SELECT clause, but you cannot use both; they are mutually exclusive.

The INSERT INTO Clause

The purpose of the INSERT INTO clause is to specify the name of the file to which you want to add records. You can specify only one file name. In this same clause, once you specify the file, you have the option of specifying which fields are to be loaded, either by their relative position within the file or by the field name.

If you choose to add records by position, you are not required to list the fields after the file name, although all the fields must be provided for within the VALUES clause or the SELECT clause. The fields will be loaded in the order in which they exist within the file.

If you choose to insert records by field names, place the names, within parentheses, after the file name. You can specify all or some of the field names, and they do not have to be in any particular order. Those fields that are not specified will be loaded with default values.

When you add records to a file, you must be sure that you do not attempt to add a record with a duplicate key, or the statement will fail.

The VALUES Clause

The VALUES clause is used to add one record to a file with set values. The order and type of the values being added must match the order and type of the fields specified in the INSERT INTO clause. For example, if a field is character, the corresponding value must be character. If a field is numeric, the corresponding value must be numeric.

The following example shows how to add a single record to a file:

1. If you want to add a record to the category master file for category 33 and a description of "Men's Apparel", you can enter either of the following two statements:

    ```
    INSERT INTO CATEGORY
    VALUES (33,'Men''s Apparel')
    ```

    ```
    INSERT INTO CATEGORY(CTDESC,CTGRY#)
    VALUES ('Men''s Apparel',33)
    ```

    The first statement enters the values by each field's relative position in the file. The second statement explicitly specifies the order of the fields in the VALUES clause.

The SELECT Clause

You use the SELECT clause when you want to add many records to a file using information from other files. The rules for the SELECT clause are the same here as when you are producing a resulting table. However, you cannot use the file name specified in the INSERT INTO clause, either directly or indirectly, anywhere in the SELECT clause. This means you cannot reference any records from the file into which you are inserting, which can at times be a drawback.

The capability to insert records into a file from another file is something that programmers often need during project development. For example, let's say you want to copy records from a production file to a test file, but you only want a specific subset of records. You can do this easily using the INSERT statement with the SELECT clause, which makes the INSERT statement a powerful tool for copying records.

Because we haven't yet discussed the more complicated features of the SELECT statement, we will show only very simple examples here. We discuss the more complex functions in connection with the INSERT statement as we come to them throughout the book.

The following examples will help you see how the INSERT statement looks and works:

1. If you want to copy every field for every record in the catalog master file in our production library into our test library, you could issue the following:

```
INSERT INTO TESTLIB/CATALOG
SELECT *  FROM PRODLIB/CATALOG
```

This statement is the same as issuing the CPYF (Copy File) command

```
CPYF PRODLIB/CATALOG TESTLIB/CATALOG MBROPT(*ADD)
```

2. Assume you have a work file that contains only a catalog number and a customer number. Now let's say you want to extract from the sales history file every unique combination of these two fields. To do so, you could issue this statement:

```
INSERT INTO WORKFILE(CATLG#,CUST#)
SELECT DISTINCT CATLG#,CUST#
  FROM SALESHST
```

THE DELETE STATEMENT

The final data manipulation statement we discuss here is the DELETE statement, which lets you delete records from a file. With the DELETE statement, you have the option to delete all the records or only those that meet certain conditions.

The DELETE statement works exactly the way you think it would. When a record meets the conditions specified, it is physically deleted from the file. Remember, however, that when you delete a record, the space in the file is still allocated. Therefore, if you are deleting all the records in a file, you would be better off using the CLRPFM (Clear Physical File Member) command instead of the DELETE statement.

The syntax for the DELETE statement is as follows:

```
DELETE     FROM <library/>file [AS] [alias]
[WHERE     predicate]
[WITH [[NC | NONE] | [UR | CHG] | [RS | ALL] | CS | RR]]
```

The DELETE FROM Clause

The DELETE FROM clause specifies the name of the file that is to have records deleted. You can specify only one file name with this clause.

The WHERE Clause

The purpose of the WHERE clause is to specify which records will be deleted. If you do not specify the WHERE clause, all records in the file will be deleted. We discuss record selection in the next chapter.

The following example shows a simple delete statement. This statement will delete every record in the category master file.

```
DELETE FROM CATEGORY
```

CHAPTER SUMMARY

SQL's data manipulation language provides AS/400 programmers with a flexible set of tools for accessing and changing a database. The biggest benefit of SQL is that you can access a database quickly without having to write programs to handle the data.

Chapter 3

Record Selection

When you process any statement in SQL's data manipulation language, you can select which records in a file are to be processed. Let's discuss the basic rules and functions that are available to help you do so. Again, remember that you can find the files and sample data we use in the examples in Appendix A.

SELECTING RECORDS

So you can select records from a file, each statement in SQL's data manipulation language provides a WHERE clause. When the WHERE clause is not specified, every record in the designated file will be processed.

The WHERE Clause

You use the WHERE clause to specify the conditions for selecting records from the file designated in the SQL statement. The format of the WHERE clause is

```
WHERE predicate
```

The predicate is any valid combination of comparison expressions. Records are selected when the WHERE clause is true.

As with any logic for selecting records, you need the capability to perform relational tests between values. The values tested can be a database field, a calculated value, or a literal. You also need the capability to perform multiple relational tests to determine whether records should be selected. The following are the available operators:

Relational Operators
=   Equal to
¬= Not equal
<> Not equal
>   Greater than
¬> Not greater than
<   Less than
¬< Not less than
>= Greater than or equal to
<= Less than or equal to

Logical Operators
AND conditioning
OR conditioning
NOT conditioning

You should avoid using the NOT symbol (¬), because it may have a different appearance in some character sets. Use an alternate operator instead (for example, use <> instead of ¬=).

You also can use parentheses to group your logic together. Therefore, you can use any combination of relational and logical operators. As an AS/400 programmer, you are probably familiar with these types of selections.

The NOT operator performs a negative test. If the condition is true, the NOT operator will make the condition false, and vice versa. When you use the NOT operator, you place it before the expression being negated. You cannot use the NOT operator with the relational operators because they already have negative operations.

1. If you do not specify the WHERE clause, all the records in a file will be selected. The following statement selects the catalog number and its description from the catalog master file. With this statement, every record is selected.

```
SELECT CATLG#,CATDSC
  FROM CATALOG
```

This statement produces the results in Table 3.1.

TABLE 3.1
Results of the Select Statement in Example 1

CATLG#	CATDSC
A597-3996A	Sahara Desert Mummy Sleeping Bag
A225-8037A	Pocket Size Cassette Player
B115-3170A	Baroque Bead Necklace
B501-1218D	Solid Leotard - Blue
C689-1192D	Knee Pants - Green
D805-0271C	Vinyl Bean Bag Chair
C871-1139C	Corduroy Bean Bag Chair
A658-4077A	Two-Person Pup Tent
A483-7921B	Case 10W40 Motor Oil
B489-7920B	Case 10W30 Motor Oil
B156-3780A	Arctic Circle Mummy Sleeping Bag
D362-7997A	Portable CD Player

2. The following statement is the same as the previous example, except that only those items in category 15 are listed:

```
SELECT CATLG#,CATDSC
  FROM CATALOG
 WHERE CTGRY# = 15
```

This statement produces the results in Table 3.2.

TABLE 3.2

Results of the Select Statement in Example 2

CATLG#	CATDSC
A597-3996A	Sahara Desert Mummy Sleeping Bag
A658-4077A	Two-Person Pup Tent
B156-3780A	Arctic Circle Mummy Sleeping Bag

3. Let's say you want to set the current year sales field to 0 in the catalog master file, but you want to do this only when the item is in category 15. To do so, you could issue the following statement, which will update three records:

```
UPDATE CATALOG
   SET CURYR$=0
 WHERE CTGRY#=15
```

Tables 3.3 and 3.4 represent, respectively, the Catalog Master File before and after this change is made.

TABLE 3.3

The Catalog Master File Before UPDATE

CATLG#	CTGRY#	CURYR$
A597-3996A	15	0.00
A225-8037A	24	4030.00
B115-3170A	38	1056.00
B501-1218D	64	3750.00
C689-1192D	64	2400.00
D805-0271C	156	1550.53
C871-1139C	156	1655.64
A658-4077A	15	1964.25
A483-7921B	348	1039.35
B489-7920B	348	1279.20
B156-3780A	15	2999.70
D362-7997A	24	270.00

TABLE 3.4

The Catalog Master File After UPDATE

CATLG#	CTGRY#	CURYR$
A597-3996A	15	0.00
A225-8037A	24	4030.00
B115-3170A	38	1056.00
B501-1218D	64	3750.00
C689-1192D	64	2400.00
D805-0271C	156	1550.53
C871-1139C	156	1655.64
A658-4077A	15	0.00
A483-7921B	348	1039.35
B489-7920B	348	1279.20
B156-3780A	15	0.00
D362-7997A	24	270.00

When the UPDATE is performed, every record that meets the conditions in the WHERE clause will be updated. This is true even if the field value in the record is the same as that specified in the SET clause (that is, even if the field already had the value you wanted to set it to).

4. If you want to delete every record in the sales history file that is before January 1, 1991, you can enter the following statement:

```
DELETE FROM SALESHST
  WHERE SHPDTE <= 901231
```

Eleven records would be deleted from the file with this statement.

5. Now let's say you want to list every catalog number and its description in the catalog master file, but you want to see only those items that are in category 15 and that have current year sales greater than $500.00. To do so, you could enter the following statement:

```
SELECT CATLG#,CATDSC
  FROM CATALOG
  WHERE CTGRY# = 15
    AND CURYR$ > 500
```

This statement will produce the results in Table 3.5.

TABLE 3.5

Results of the Select Statement in Example 5

CATLG#	CATDSC
A658-4077A	Two-Person Pup Tent
B156-3780A	Arctic Circle Mummy Sleeping Bag

6. If you want to copy records from the catalog master file in production into a test library and you are interested only in those items that had sales figures of more than $500.00 for all three years, you can enter the following:

```
INSERT INTO TESTLIB/CATALOG
SELECT *
  FROM PRODLIB/CATALOG
 WHERE CURYR$>500
   AND YR1$>500
   AND YR2$>500
```

This statement produces the results in Table 3.6.

TABLE 3.6

Records Inserted into TESTLIB/CATALOG

CATLG#	...
A225-8037A	...
B115-3170A	...
B501-1218D	...
C689-1192D	...
A658-4077A	...

7. To select the catalog and category number for every record in the catalog master file that is in category 15, and where any of the sales figures are 0, you could enter the following statement:

```
SELECT CATLG#,CTGRY#
  FROM CATALOG
 WHERE CTGRY# = 15
   AND (CURYR$ = 0 OR YR1$ = 0 OR YR2$ = 0)
```

This statement produces the results in Table 3.7.

TABLE 3.7
Results of the Select Statement in Example 7

CATLG#	CTGRY#
A597-3996A	15
B156-3780A	15

8. If you want to list every catalog and category number in the catalog master file that is not in category 15, you could enter one of the following:

```
SELECT CATLG#,CTGRY#
  FROM CATALOG
 WHERE NOT CTGRY# = 15
SELECT CATLG#,CTGRY#
  FROM CATALOG
 WHERE CTGRY# ¬ = 15
```

These statements produce the results in Table 3.8.

TABLE 3.8
Results of the Select Statements in Example 8

CATLG#	CTGRY#
A225-8037A	24
B115-3170A	38
B501-1218D	64
C689-1192D	64
D805-0271C	156
C871-1139C	156
A483-7921B	348
B489-7920B	348
D362-7997A	24

9. Finally, if you want to select the catalog and category number from the catalog master file, and you only want those records that are in category 15 and that do not have any sales figures equal to 0, you can enter the following statement:

```
SELECT CATLG#,CTGRY#
  FROM CATALOG
 WHERE CTGRY# = 15
   AND NOT (CURYR$ = 0 OR YR1$ = 0 OR YR2$ = 0)
```

This statement produces the results in Table 3.9.

TABLE **3.9**
Results of the Select Statement in Example 9

CATLG#	CTGRY#
A658-4077A	15

SPECIAL OPERATORS

In addition to the relational and logical operators presented here, SQL provides some other operators for selecting records. Using these special operators will greatly enhance your ability to select records in a way that is easy to understand. Following are some of those special operators and how they are used.

The BETWEEN Operator

The BETWEEN operator lets you test whether a value or expression is between two different values, inclusively. The value you use can be any field or a calculated value. This operator is valid for numeric, character, and date values.

The syntax of the BETWEEN operator is

```
expression [NOT] BETWEEN expression AND expression
```

You are responsible for ensuring that the range specified is valid. If the second value (after the AND) is less than the first value, no records would be selected, but no error is indicated when this occurs.

The BETWEEN operator also lets you negate the BETWEEN test. In other words, if the range test was true and you use the NOT keyword, the result will be false, and vice versa.

1. Let's say you want to list every catalog number in the catalog master file where the category number is between 1 and 100. To do so, you could enter the following statement:

```
SELECT CATLG#,CATDSC
  FROM CATALOG
 WHERE CTGRY# BETWEEN 1 AND 100
```

This test would be the same as saying

```
 WHERE CTGRY# >= 1 AND CTGRY# <= 100
```

The above statements produce the results in Table 3.10.

TABLE 3.10

Results of the Select Statements in Example 1

CATLG#	CATDSC
A597-3996A	Sahara Desert Mummy Sleeping Bag
A225-8037A	Pocket Size Cassette Player
B115-3170A	Baroque Bead Necklace
B501-1218D	Solid Leotard - Blue
C689-1192D	Knee Pants - Green
A658-4077A	Two-Person Pup Tent
B156-3780A	Arctic Circle Mummy Sleeping Bag
D362-7997A	Portable CD Player

2. Now let's say you want to list every catalog number in the catalog master file where there has been a progressive increase in sales for each of the years available. To do this, you can enter the following statement:

```
SELECT CATLG#,CATDSC
  FROM CATALOG
 WHERE YR1$ BETWEEN YR2$ AND CURYR$
```

This would be the same as saying

```
 WHERE YR1$ >= YR2$
   AND YR1$ <= CURYR$
```

These statements produce the results in Table 3.11.

TABLE 3.11

Results of the Select Statements in Example 2

CATLG#	CATDSC
D362-7997A	Portable CD Player

3. Now let's assume you want to list each customer number and name in the customer master file where the Zip code starts with 44. You could enter the following statement to accomplish this:

```
SELECT CUST#,NAME
  FROM CUSTMAST
WHERE ZIP BETWEEN '44' AND '44999-9999'
```

This statement produces the results in Table 3.12.

TABLE 3.12
Results of the Select Statement in Example 3

CUST#	NAME
411	Bob & Carol's Hallway Gifts
32418	Hemingway Travel Club

4. Finally, let's say you want to perform the same test as in example 3, except you want to know which customers do not have a Zip code that begins with 44. To do this, you could enter the following statement:

```
SELECT CUST#,NAME
  FROM CUSTMAST
WHERE ZIP NOT BETWEEN '44' AND '44999-9999'
```

This statement produces the results in Table 3.13.

TABLE 3.13
Results of the Select Statement in Example 4

CUST#	NAME
392	Jane's Gift Emporium
1583	Paul's Auto Store
8395	Alice's Sundries
62990	Bar & Grill Health Club

The IN Operator

The IN operator lets you test a field against a list of values. You can provide the list of values, or it can be derived from a subselect. We cover the subselect in Chapter 7. For now, we show the IN operator with a static list of values.

The syntax of the IN operator is

```
expression [NOT] IN ({expression,... | Sub-SELECT})
```

This operator is valid for numeric, character, and date values. When you provide the values to be tested, those values must be separated by commas. Character values must be surrounded by apostrophes.

Following are some simple examples using the IN operator.

1. If you want to list every customer from the customer master file that is in the state of Ohio, California, Wisconsin, or North Carolina, you could enter the following statement:

```
SELECT CUST#,NAME
  FROM CUSTMAST
WHERE STATE IN ('OH','CA','WI','NC')
```

This statement produces the results in Table 3.14.

TABLE 3.14
Results of the Select Statement in Example 1

CUST#	NAME
411	Bob & Carol's Hallway Gifts
8395	Alice's Sundries
32418	Hemingway Travel Club

2. Now let's say you want to list every item in the catalog master file that is in any of the following categories: 15, 38, or 156. To do so, you could enter the following statement:

```
SELECT CATLG#,CATDSC
  FROM CATALOG
WHERE CTGRY# IN (15,38,156)
```

This statement produces the results in Table 3.15.

TABLE 3.15
Results of the Select Statement in Example 2

CATLG#	CATDSC
A597-3996A	Sahara Desert Mummy Sleeping Bag
B115-3170A	Baroque Bead Necklace
D805-0271C	Vinyl Bean Bag Chair
C871-1139C	Corduroy Bean Bag Chair
A658-4077A	Two-Person Pup Tent
B156-3780A	Arctic Circle Mummy Sleeping Bag

3. Finally, let's say you want to list every customer that is not in any of the following states: Ohio, California, Wisconsin, or North Carolina. To do so,

you could use this statement:

```
SELECT CUST#,NAME
  FROM CUSTMAST
  WHERE STATE NOT IN ('OH','CA','WI','NC')
```

This statement produces the results in Table 3.16.

TABLE 3.16

Results of the Select Statement in Example 3

CUST#	NAME
392	Jane's Gift Emporium
1583	Paul's Auto Store
62990	Bar & Grill Health Club

The LIKE Operator

The LIKE operator lets you test a string value to see whether it contains certain characters. This process is similar to a scan function. The LIKE operator is valid only with character values.

The syntax of the LIKE operator is

```
expression [NOT] LIKE {'search characters' | USER |
    CURRENT SERVER} [ESCAPE 'character']
```

Two special characters are used to specify how to look for characters within a string. The first special character is %, which indicates any number of missing characters. The second special character is _, which indicates one missing character only. By combining % and _, you can find any combination of characters.

One thing to keep in mind about the LIKE function is that ending spaces are considered significant to this function. Therefore, when you use the LIKE function against a fixed-length field, the only way to find the last characters is by using the % after the value for which you are searching — unless you use the STRIP built-in function, which we describe in Chapter 4.

If you are using the LIKE function against a variable-length field, you can find the ending values by first using the % character and then using the search characters.

When you are using the LIKE operator, you must remember that the test is case sensitive. The TRANSLATE, UCASE, or UPPER built-in functions, which we discuss in Chapter 4, can be used to convert a character string to uppercase to help avoid situations where case sensitivity is a problem.

THE **ESCAPE** CLAUSE

The purpose of the ESCAPE clause is to assist you in searching for the characters % and _. Because these special characters are interpreted as wild-card characters, you need a method to indicate when they are not to be used as wild cards.

The format of the ESCAPE clause is

```
ESCAPE 'character'
```

The character you specify must be only one character in length and enclosed within single quotation marks ('). This character is then specified within the search characters just before the % or _ character. For example,

```
LIKE 'ABC+%' ESCAPE '+'
```

would search for the characters ABC%, not any string that started with ABC.

If you specify the same escape character twice in a row within the search characters, this indicates that you are searching for the actual character specified. For example,

```
LIKE '++ABC+%' ESCAPE '+'
```

would search for the characters +ABC%.

The LIKE operator also provides you with the capability to negate the test. If the LIKE operator proves true, the NOT operator will make the result false, and vice versa.

In the following examples, you will want to pay close attention to the data examples to see how the LIKE operator works.

1. If you want to know every catalog number within the catalog master file that contains the letters Bag in the description field, you could enter the following statement:

```
SELECT CATLG#, CATDSC
  FROM CATALOG
 WHERE CATDSC LIKE '%Bag%'
```

This statement produces the results in Table 3.17.

TABLE 3.17
Results of the Select Statement in Example 1

CATLG#	CATDSC
A597-3996A	Sahara Desert Mummy Sleeping Bag
D805-0271C	Vinyl Bean Bag Chair
C871-1139C	Corduroy Bean Bag Chair
B156-3780A	Arctic Circle Mummy Sleeping Bag

This test checks to see whether there are any number of characters, the letters Bag, then any number of characters.

2. The following statement would give different results, depending on whether the description field is a fixed- or variable-length field. First, let's assume the field is a fixed-length field.

```
SELECT CATLG#,CATDSC
  FROM CATALOG
 WHERE CATDSC LIKE '%Bag'
```

Because the field is a fixed length, the results of this test would prduce a table with no records, as shown below in Table 3.18, because ending spaces in a fixed-length field are considered significant.

TABLE 3.18
Results of the Select Statement in Example 2

CATLG#	CATDSC
No records selected	

In Table 3.19, note what happens if you execute the same statement, except that this time the field is a variable-length field.

TABLE 3.19
Results of the Select Statement with a Variable-Length Field

CATLG#	CATDSC
A597-3996A	Sahara Desert Mummy Sleeping Bag
B156-3780A	Arctic Circle Mummy Sleeping Bag

3. The following statement will find all the catalog items from the catalog master file where the description begins with the letters Case.

```
SELECT CATLG#,CATDSC
  FROM CATALOG
 WHERE CATDSC LIKE 'Case%'
```

This statement produces the results in Table 3.20.

TABLE 3.20
Results of the Select Statement in Example 3

CATLG#	CATDSC
A483-7921B	Case 10W40 Motor Oil
B489-7920B	Case 10W30 Motor Oil

4. The following is an example of selecting all the catalog items in the catalog master file where the description has one character, then the letter o, then any number of characters, then the letters ay, then any number of characters.

```
SELECT CATLG#,CATDSC
  FROM CATALOG
  WHERE CATDSC LIKE '_o%ay%'
```

This statement produces the results in Table 3.21.

TABLE 3.21
Results of the Select Statement in Example 4

CATLG#	CATDSC
A225-8037A	Pocket Size Cassette Player
D362-7997A	Portable CD Player

5. Finally, let's say you want to know which items in the catalog master file do not have the letters Bag in the description field. To find out, you can enter the following statement:

```
SELECT CATLG#,CATDSC
  FROM CATALOG
  WHERE CATDSC NOT LIKE '%Bag%'
```

This statement produces the results in Table 3.22.

TABLE 3.22
Results of the Select Statement in Example 5

CATLG#	CATDSC
A225-8037A	Pocket Size Cassette Player
B115-3170A	Baroque Bead Necklace
B501-1218D	Solid Leotard - Blue
C689-1192D	Knee Pants - Green
A658-4077A	Two-Person Pup Tent
A483-7921B	Case 10W40 Motor Oil
B489-7920B	Case 10W30 Motor Oil
D362-7997A	Portable CD Player

The NULL Operator

The NULL operator lets you test whether a null-capable field contains a null value. This test is helpful if you want to exclude null values from being processed, which is especially useful when those fields are used in calculations within the statement. Remember, any calculation using a field that contains a null value always results in a null value.

The NULL operator also lets you negate the result. If the null test is true and you use the NOT keyword, the result will be false, and vice versa.

The format of the NULL operator is

```
expression IS [NOT] NULL
```

The following examples show you how the NULL operator works. Assume that our catalog master file allows for null values in the future price field (FPRICE). Also assume that any record in our table that contains a 0 in this field is actually a null value.

1. Let's say you want to list every item in the catalog master file that contains a null value in the future price field. To do so, you can enter the following statement:

```
SELECT CATLG#,CATDSC
  FROM CATALOG
 WHERE FPRICE IS NULL
```

This statement produces the results in Table 3.23.

TABLE 3.23
Results of the Select Statement in Example 1

CATLG#	CATDSC
A597-3996A	Sahara Desert Mummy Sleeping Bag
A225-8037A	Pocket Size Cassette Player
B115-3170A	Baroque Bead Necklace
B501-1218D	Solid Leotard - Blue
C689-1192D	Knee Pants - Green
C871-1139C	Corduroy Bean Bag Chair
A658-4077A	Two-Person Pup Tent
A483-7921B	Case 10W40 Motor Oil
B489-7920B	Case 10W30 Motor Oil
D362-7997A	Portable CD Player

2. Now let's say you want only those items that do not contain a null value. You can enter the same statement as above, except this time use the NOT keyword to negate the test.

```
SELECT CATLG#,CATDSC
  FROM CATALOG
  WHERE FPRICE IS NOT NULL
```

This statement produces the results in Table 3.24.

TABLE 3.24

Results of the Select Statement in Example 2

CATLG#	CATDSC
D805-0271C	Vinyl Bean Bag Chair
B156-3780A	Arctic Circle Mummy Sleeping Bag

CHAPTER SUMMARY

As you can see, the WHERE clause provides a powerful mechanism for selecting records. You can use any combination of the relational, logical, and special operators that we have presented so far. There are additional special operators, but we will explain these during our discussion about subselect processing in Chapter 7.

Chapter 4

Built-in Functions

SQL provides many built-in functions that let you change how data is presented. These functions are of two types: scalar and column. We discuss scalar functions here and column functions in the next chapter.

SCALAR FUNCTIONS

Scalar functions let you change the size and characteristics of a field or perform arithmetic operations against a field. You can perform some scalar functions on numeric values, some on character values, and others on date values.

You can use scalar functions anywhere a valid expression is allowed. This means you can use them when you are selecting fields, testing values, or even when you are updating a field in a database file. Scalar functions also can be embedded within each other as long as you maintain the data types and follow the rules.

The ABSVAL Function

The ABSVAL function returns the absolute value for a number. The syntax of the ABSVAL function is

```
ABSVAL(expression) or ABS(expression)
```

1. Let's assume a field called AMOUNT contains a value of -1000. In this case,

```
ABSVAL(AMOUNT)
```

will return a value of 1000.

2. If AMOUNT contains a value of 1000, the above function still will return a value of 1000.

The CASE Function

The CASE function is a special function used to return a single value based on a series of tests. The syntax of the CASE function is

```
CASE (search clause | simple when) ELSE (NULL | expression) END

Search clause:  WHEN  search-condition THEN NULL | expression
Simple when:    expression WHEN expression THEN NULL |
     expression
```

With a simple WHEN condition, you specify an expression and each WHEN clause is compared against the expression. When a match is found, the value specified after the THEN clause is returned.

With a search clause, you specify the test conditions within the WHEN clause. When the result is true, the value specified in the THEN clause is returned. Below are several examples using the CASE function.

```
CASE DEPTFLAG
          WHEN '1' THEN 'Operations'
          WHEN '2' THEN 'Network Administration'
          WHEN '3' THEN 'Programming'
          WHEN '4' THEN 'Engineering'
          WHEN '5' THEN 'Security'
     ELSE 'Unknown'
     END

CASE
          WHEN DEPTFLAG = '1' THEN 'Operations'
          WHEN DEPTFLAG = '2' THEN 'Network Administration'
          WHEN DEPTFLAG = '3' THEN 'Programming'
          WHEN DEPTFLAG = '4' THEN 'Engineering'
          WHEN DEPTFLAG = '5' THEN 'Security'
     ELSE 'Unknown'
     END

SELECT *
   FROM EMPLOYEE
 WHERE (CASE  WHEN SALARY = 0 THEN NULL
                            ELSE SALARY+COMM$
              END) > 10,000
```

The CAST Function

The CAST function is used to change the attribute of a field during execution of the SQL statement. The syntax of the CAST function is

```
CAST expression AS data-type | NULL
```

You can change numeric to character, character to numeric, characters to dates, dates to character, and so on. This is useful when you are populating another database with information and you need to change the attributes to match the new database field definition. The CAST function does not change the original database field definition.

The following list provides information about the valid data types:

INTEGER — defines a large integer value.

INT — the same as INTEGER.

SMALLINT — defines a small integer value.

FLOAT [(precision)] — defines a floating-point value. If the precision is not entered or contains a value between 25 and 53, the number will be a double-precision, floating-point number. If the precision is between 1 and 24, the number will be a single-precision, floating-point number.

REAL — defines a single-precision, floating-point number.

DOUBLE PRECISION — defines a double-precision, floating-point number.

DOUBLE — the same as DOUBLE PRECISION.

DECIMAL [(length [,decimals])] — defines a packed-decimal field. If you do not specify the length of the number, the default will be 5 with 0 decimals. If you specify the length but do not specify the decimals, the default will be 0 decimals. The length can be any value between 1 and 31. If you specify both the length and the decimals, the decimals cannot be greater than the length of the number.

DEC — the same as DECIMAL.

NUMERIC [(length [,decimals])] — defines a zoned-decimal field. If you do not specify the length of the number, the default will be 5 with 0 decimals. If you specify the length but do not specify the decimals, the default will be 0 decimals. The length can be any value between 1 and 31. If you specify both the length and the decimals, the decimals cannot be greater than the length of the number.

CHARACTER [(length)] [FOR BIT DATA |
> **FOR SBCS DATA |**
> **FOR MIXED DATA ccsid]** — defines a fixed-length
character value. If you do not specify the length, the default will be 1. The length specified can be any value between 1 and 32,766.

The second argument of this definition indicates the type of data that can be stored in this character field. FOR BIT DATA specifies that the data is not associated with any coded character sets and that character conversions are never performed. FOR SBCS DATA refers to a field that is stored using single-byte character set (SBCS) data representations. FOR MIXED DATA is used for a field that can contain both SBCS and double-byte character set (DBCS) data. With this argument, you must specify a valid coded-character-set identifier (CCSID).

CHAR — the same as CHARACTER.

VARCHAR (length) [ALLOCATE (length)]
> **[FOR BIT DATA |**
> **FOR SBCS DATA |**
> **FOR MIXED DATA ccsid]** — defines a variable-length character string.
You must specify a length between 1 and 32,740.

The ALLOCATE keyword tells how much space should be reserved for the field within the database record. When a character value is stored and it is less than the allocated size, the data is stored in the fixed portion of the database record. If the string is longer than the allocated size, the data is stored in the variable location for the record and requires more I/O to retrieve the record. If you do not specify an allocated length, the default is 0.

The second argument of this definition indicates the type of data that can be stored in this character field.

FOR BIT DATA specifies that the data is not associated with any coded character sets and that character conversions are never performed.

FOR SBCS DATA refers to a field that is stored using SBCS data representations.

FOR MIXED DATA refers to a field that can contain both SBCS and DBCS data. With this argument, you must specify a valid CCSID.

CHARACTER VARYING — the same as VARCHAR.

CHAR VARYING — the same as VARCHAR.

LONG VARCHAR — defines the field as a variable-length character field whose length is determined by the amount of space available for the row. The maximum length for a single row is 32,766 characters. If there are any variable-length fields defined in the row, the maximum length is 32,740 characters.

GRAPHIC [(length)] — defines a field as a DBCS field. If you do not specify the length, the default is 1. The length specified can be any value between 1 and 16,383. If the field is null-capable, the maximum length is 16,382 characters.

VARGRAPHIC (length) [ALLOCATE (length)] — defines a field as a variable-length DBCS field. You must specify a length and the value must be between 1 and 16,370. If the field is null-capable, the maximum length is 16,369 characters.

The ALLOCATE keyword designates the space to be reserved for the field within the database record. When a graphic character is stored that is less than the allocated size, the data is stored within a fixed portion of the database record. If the string is longer than the allocated size, the data is stored in the variable location for the record (more I/O is required for retrieving this data). If you do not specify an allocated size, the default is 0.

GRAPHIC VARYING — the same as VARGRAPHIC.

LONG VARGRAPHIC — defines the field as a variable-length graphic field whose length is determined by the amount of space available for the row. The maximum length for a single row is 32,766 characters. If there are any variable-length fields defined in the row, the maximum length is 32,740 characters.

DATE — defines a date field in ISO format (yyyy-mm-dd).

TIME — defines a time field in ISO format (hh.mm.ss).

TIMESTAMP — defines a timestamp field.

Here is an example of the CAST function:

```
SELECT CAST(SALARY AS INTEGER)
          FROM EMPLOYEE
```

The CHAR Function

The CHAR function converts a date, time, or timestamp into a valid character string, a numeric value into a character string, or a character string into a character string. The syntax of the CHAR function are

```
CHAR(date expression [,ISO | ,USA | ,EUR | JIS]
CHAR(character expression [,integer])
CHAR(integer expression)
CHAR(decimal expression [,decimal character]
CHAR(floating-point expression [,decimal character]
```

When you specify the date version of this function, the result will be in the format specified when the second operand is expressed. However, the second operand is not allowed when the value is a timestamp. If the second operand is not specified, the format of the date value and the separators used is based on the environment in which the SQL statement is executing.

Table 4.1 shows the result for each format allowed.

TABLE 4.1
Results for Allowed Formats

Data Type	Value	Format	Result
DATE	07/29/99	ISO	1999-07-29
		USA	07/29/1999
		EUR	29.07.1999
		JIS	1999-07-29
TIME	13:14:59	ISO	13.14.59
		USA	1:14 PM
		EUR	13.14.59
		JIS	13:14:59
TIMESTAMP	1999-07-29-13.14.59	N/A	1999-07-29-13.14.59.000000

When you specify the character version of this function, you will specify a character expression and then an optional integer value indicating the desired length of the new character value.

When you specify the integer version of this function, you will specify an integer value. The result will be the character equivalent of the integer.

When you specify the decimal or floating-point version of this function, you will specify either a decimal or floating-point expression. You can optionally specify what character is to be used to represent the decimal point.

The CHARACTER_LENGTH Function

The CHARACTER_LENGTH function returns the length of a string value. The length returned includes blanks, unless the string is a variable-length string. The syntax of the CHARACTER_LENGTH function is

```
CHARACTER_LENGTH(expression) or CHAR_LENGTH(expression)
```

This function is similar to the LENGTH function, except that this function is valid only for character values.

1. Let's assume a field called ADDR is 30 bytes long and contains a value of 123 MAIN ST. In this case,

```
CHARACTER_LENGTH(ADDR)
```

will return a value of 30.

2. Now assume that ADDR is a variable-length field. The above function will return a value of 12.

The COALESE Function

You use the COALESE function in connection with null values to return the value of the first expression that is not null. You are required to have at least two values specified in this function. The COALESE function is the same as the VALUE function; it is also similar to the IFNULL function. The COALESE function is valid for any data type. The syntax of this function is

```
COALESE(expression, expression [,expression ...])
```

As you probably remember, when a field contains a null value and is used in an arithmetic operation, the result is a null value. The COALESE function lets you override this feature. If all the expressions listed in this function are null values, the result is a null value.

Each expression used in the COALESE function must be of the same type. For example, if any expression is a date, every expression must be a date; if any expression is numeric, every expression must be numeric. The result of the function is converted to the size of the maximum value contained within the function.

1. If you have a numeric field called FIELD and it is possible for this field to contain null values, and you want to use this field in a calculation, you can enter the following function:

```
COALESE(FIELD, 0)
```

If the field contains a value, that value is returned first. If the value is null, the function returns a 0.

The CONCAT Function

The CONCAT function takes two character-string values and creates a single character-string value. This function is the same as the CONCAT (| |) operator. The syntax of the CONCAT function is

```
CONCAT(expression, expression)
```

This function does not truncate or pad values, so trailing blanks are included in the result. However, if the string values are variable-length values, only the actual values are concatenated.

1. Let's assume you have two fields called FNAME and LNAME, each 15 characters in length. In this case,

```
CONCAT(FNAME,LNAME)
```

results in a character string 30 bytes long.

2. If both fields are variable-length fields, the result is dependent on the values contained in the fields.

The CURDATE Function

The CURDATE function returns a date based on the current system date where the application is executing. This function is the same as the CURRENT_DATE special register. The syntax of the CURDATE function is

```
CURDATE()
```

This function has no specified arguments. However, you are required to specify the parentheses. The syntax of the date returned is based on the environment in which the function is executed.

The CURTIME Function

The CURTIME function returns a time based on the current system time where the application is executing. This function is the same as the CURRENT_TIME special register. The syntax of the CURTIME function is

```
CURTIME()
```

This function has no specified arguments. However, you are required to specify the parentheses. The syntax of the time returned is based on the environment in which the function is executed.

The DATE Function

The DATE function returns a date value from the specified expression. The syntax of the DATE function is

```
DATE(expression)
```

The expression can be a timestamp, a date, a string representation of a date, a character string of length 7, or a positive number. In each case, the value returned will be the date portion of the expression.

The date will be in the ISO format. A timestamp value results in only the date portion of the timestamp being returned. The string representation of a date refers to any string value that would be valid in a date field.

The character string of length 7 represents a date in the form of *yyyynnn*, where *yyyy* equals the year and *nnn* equals the Julian day of that year. The positive number can be any value between 1 and 3652059. This number represents an absolute number for any date between January 1, 1 A.D. and December 31, 9999 A.D. This is the opposite of the DAYS function.

1. Assume that a field called CATDTE is defined as a timestamp field and contains a value of 1999-08-14-15.45.32.145245. In this case,

   ```
   DATE(CATDTE)
   ```

   will return a value of 1999-08-14.

2. You also can code the DATE function with a numeric value. For example,

   ```
   DATE(727257)
   ```

   will return a value of 1992-02-29.

The DAY Function

The DAY function returns the day portion of a date, timestamp, date duration, or timestamp duration. The result will be an integer value. If the expression contains a null value, the result will be a null value. The syntax of the DAY function is

```
DAY(expression)
```

When a date or timestamp is used, the value returned will be between 1 and 31. When a date duration or timestamp duration is used, the result will be a value between -99 and 99.

1. Assume that a field called CATDTE is defined as a date field and contains a value of 1999-08-14. In this case,

   ```
   DAY(CATDTE)
   ```

   will return a value of 14.

2. Assume that two fields are defined as timestamp fields and are called SLDDTE and CATDTE. SLDDTE has a value of 1999-08-14-15.45.32.145245 and CATDTE has a value of 1999-01-01-16.33.24.432543. In this case,

   ```
   DAY(SLDDTE-CATDTE)
   ```

   will return a value of 12.

The DAYOFMONTH Function

The DAYOFMONTH function is exactly the same as the DAY function. This means that this function returns the day portion of a date, timestamp, date duration, or timestamp duration. The result is an integer value. If the expression contains a null value, the result will be a null value. The syntax for the DAYOFMONTH function is

`DAYOFMONTH(expression)`

When you use a date or timestamp, the value returned will be between 1 and 31. When you use a date duration or a timestamp duration, the result will be a value between -99 and 99.

The DAYOFWEEK Function

The DAYOFWEEK function returns an integer value that represents the day of the week for a date. The values returned will be from 1 to 7, with 1 being Sunday and 7 being Saturday. The syntax for the DAYOFWEEK function is

`DAYOFWEEK(expression)`

The expression within this function must be either a date or a timestamp value. If the expression results in a null value, the result of this function will be a null value.

1. Let's assume a date field called DATE contains a value of 1996-10-20. In this case,

`DAYOFWEEK(DATE)`

will return a value of 1.

The DAYOFYEAR Function

The DAYOFYEAR function returns an integer value that represents the Julian day of the year for a date. The values returned are from 1 to 366. The syntax for the DAYOFYEAR function is

`DAYOFYEAR(expression)`

The expression within this function must be either a date or a timestamp value. If the expression results in a null value, the result of this function will be a null value.

1. Let's assume a date field called DATE contains a value of 1996-10-20. In this case,

`DAYOFYEAR(DATE)`

will return a value of 284.

The DAYS Function

The DAYS function returns an integer value of a date. This value is the number of days since January 1, 1 A.D. You can think of this as an absolute number of a date value. The DAYS function is the opposite of the DATE function. The syntax of the DAYS function is

```
DAYS(expression)
```

The expression must be a date, a timestamp, or a valid string representation of a date value. If the expression contains a null value, the result will be a null value.

1. Assume that a field called CATDTE is defined as a date field and contains a value of 1992-08-14. In this case,

```
DAYS(CATDTE)
```

will return a value of 727424.

One word of caution is in order here: It is very easy to confuse the DAY and DAYS functions.

The DECIMAL Function

The DECIMAL function converts an expression to a decimal value so you can define the size of the decimal value, which is useful when you want to present a calculated value with a specific size instead of the default size. You might need to do this when you are performing an INSERT into a file or when you are printing a list and want the results to have the proper number of decimals.

You can also use the DECIMAL function to convert a character string to a decimal value. In this case, you must ensure that the character string contains a valid representation of a decimal value. When specifying this function, you must specify which character represents the decimal point if the number contained in the character string contains a decimal character other than a period. The syntax of the DECIMAL function is

```
DECIMAL(expression, size, decimals)
```

```
DECIMAL(character expression, size, decimals, decimal character)
```

You also can round values using the DECIMAL function. You do this by adding to the value a figure exactly one decimal place longer than the final result value. For example, if the number of decimals is 2 and you want to perform half-adjusting, you would add .005 to the calculation. If the number of decimals is 0 and you want to round up if there is any fractional value, you would add .9999 to the calculated value, the number of 9s depending on the accuracy you want for rounding up.

With the DECIMAL function, you must be careful that significant digits are not truncated when you are sizing the value. If this happens, the statement being executed will fail. And finally, if any field in the expression contains a null value, the result will be a null value.

The following examples show the result of using the DECIMAL function.

1. Let's assume that we have two fields called ORDQTY (order quantity) and PRICE (order price) and we want to multiply them together; however, we want the result to have a size of 9.2. In this case,

```
DECIMAL(ORDQTY*PRICE,9,2)
```

would do this for us.

If ORDQTY has a value of 300 and PRICE has a value of 15.99, the result will be 4797.00.

2. Now assume that we want to divide a field AMOUNT (amount sold) by SHPQTY (quantity shipped), but we want to round up using half-adjustment. We could enter

```
DECIMAL(AMOUNT/SHPQTY+.005,9,2)
```

If AMOUNT has a value of 435.77 and SHPQTY has a value of 23, the result will be 18.95.

3. Assume that we want to convert a character value to a numeric value. We could enter

```
DECIMAL('123.45',5,2)
```

The numeric value returned will contain the value of 123.45.

The DIGITS Function

The DIGITS function converts a number into a character value. The value converted will be the absolute value of the number in the expression. Also, leading zeros are put in the result based on the size of the fields in the expression.

The syntax of the DIGITS function is

```
DIGITS(expression)
```

If any field in the expression contains a null value, the result will be a null value.

1. Let's assume we have a field called CATDTE (catalog entry date) that is 6 digits long with 0 decimals and that has a value of 31689. In this case,

```
DIGITS(CATDTE)
```

will result in a value of 031689.

The DOUBLE_PRECISION Function

The DOUBLE_PRECISION function lets you convert a number or a character representation of a number into a double-precision, floating-point number. This function is the same as the FLOAT function. The syntax of this function is

```
DOUBLE_PRECISION(expression) or DOUBLE(expression)
DOUBLE(character expression,)
```

If any field in the expression is a null value, the result will be a null value.

1. Let's assume that we want to divide a field called AMOUNT (amount sold) by a field called SHPQTY (shipped quantity), but we want the result to be a floating-point value. To accomplish this, we can enter the following statement:

```
DOUBLE_PRECISION(AMOUNT/SHPQTY)
```

If AMOUNT contains a value of 435.77 and SHPQTY contains a value of 23, the above statement will return a value of 1.8946521739130436E+001.

The FLOAT Function

The FLOAT function lets you convert a number or a character representation of a number into a floating-point decimal number. The FLOAT function is the same as the DOUBLE_PRECISION function. The syntax of this function is

```
FLOAT(expression)
FLOAT(character expression)
```

The result is a double-precision, floating-point number. If any field in the expression is a null value, the result will be a null value. For example,

1. Let's assume that we wish to divide a field called AMOUNT (amount sold) by a field called SHPQTY (shipped quantity), but we want the result to be a floating-point value. To accomplish this, we could enter the following statement:

```
FLOAT(AMOUNT/SHPQTY)
```

If AMOUNT contains a value of 435.77 and SHPQTY contains a value of 23, the above statement will return a value of 1.8946521739130436E+001.

The FLOOR Function

The FLOOR function lets you convert a number into its integer equivalent. This function is the same as the INTEGER function. Converting a number into its integer form means that decimals are truncated. The syntax of the FLOOR function is

```
FLOOR(expression)
```

The result of this function is always a large integer value. The value of the expression must be between -21474836448 and 2147483647, inclusive.

1. Let's assume a field called PRICE contains a value of 102.99. In this case,

```
FLOOR(PRICE)
```

will return a value of 102.

The HASH Function

The HASH function returns the partition number for a set of values. This function lets you determine what the partition number will be if the partitioning key is composed of the values in the expression. For a discussion of partition keys and the HASH function, see Chapter 8.

The HEX Function

The HEX function returns the hexadecimal equivalent of a value. The length of the result will be twice that of the value being converted. The first two digits will represent the first byte of the value, the next two digits will represent the second byte, and so forth. The syntax of the HEX function is

```
HEX(expression)
```

Any data type is valid with the HEX function. If the expression contains a null value, the result will be a null value.

1. If you are using the HEX function with a value of 'ABC',

```
HEX('ABC')
```

will return a value of C1C2C3.

The HOUR Function

The HOUR function returns the hour portion of a time, timestamp, time duration, or timestamp duration. The result will be an integer value. If the expression contains a null value, the result will be a null value. The syntax of the HOUR function is

```
HOUR(expression)
```

The return value will be between 0 and 24 if you use a time or timestamp value. If you use a time or timestamp duration, the result will be a value between -99 and 99.

1. Assume that a field called MNTTIM is defined as a time field and contains a value of 13:23:45. In this case,

```
HOUR(MNTTIM)
```

will return a value of 13.

2. Assume that two fields are defined as timestamp fields and are called SLDDTE and CATDTE. SLDDTE has a value of 1999-08-14-15.45.32.145245 and CATDTE has a value of 1999-01-01-16.33.24.432543. In this case,

```
HOUR(SLDDTE-CATDTE)
```

will return a value of 23.

The IFNULL Function

The IFNULL function is the same as the COALESE and VALUE functions, except that only two values are allowed with the IFNULL function. You use this function to compare values against a null value and return the first one value that is not null. The syntax of the IFNULL function is

```
IFNULL(expression, expression)
```

If both expressions in this function are null values, the result is a null value. Also, both expressions must be of the same data type.

1. Assume you have a numeric field called FIELD and it is possible for this field to contain null values. For the following expression, if the field contains a value,

```
IFNULL(FIELD, 0)
```

that value is returned first. If the value of the field is null, then the function returns a 0.

The INTEGER Function

The INTEGER function lets you convert a number or a character representation of a number into its integer equivalent, truncating the decimal positions. When you use the INTEGER function, the result is always a large integer value and any decimal positions are truncated. The maximum value of the expression is 2147483647 and the minimum value is -21474836448.

The syntax of the INTEGER function is

```
INTEGER(expression)
INTEGER(character expression)
```

1. Let's assume a field called PRICE contains a value of 102.99. In this case,

```
INTEGER(PRICE)
```

will return a value of 102.

The LEFT Function

The LEFT function returns the leftmost characters of a specified string value. If you are using this function interactively or with Query Manager, the length specified must be an integer value and must be greater than zero. When you use this function within a program, you can have a zero value for the length as long as the host variable is defined as a binary integer. For a discussion of host variables, see Chapter 10.

The syntax of the LEFT function is

```
LEFT(expression, length)
```

If the length specified is greater than the actual length of the string, the string is padded with blanks to make up the length specified.

1. Let's assume a field called ADDR contains a value of "123 Main St.". In this case,

```
LEFT(ADDR,5)
```

will return a value of "123 M".

2. Assume that ADDR is defined with a length of 12. In this case,

```
LEFT(ADDR,15)
```

will return a value of "123 Main St.   ". Notice the extra blanks.

The LENGTH Function

The LENGTH function returns the length of a value. The length returned is a number and represents the number of positions that are required to store the value. The value checked can be either a numeric, a character, or a date value. If the value is a fixed-length character string, trailing blanks are included in the length returned.

The syntax of the LENGTH function is

```
LENGTH(expression)
```

Table 4.2 shows what you can expect to be returned, depending on what type of value you are checking.

TABLE 4.2
Results of the Length Function

Length	Data Type
2	SMALL INTEGER
4	LARGE INTEGER
4	SINGLE-PRECISION FLOATING POINT
8	DOUBLE-PRECISION FLOATING POINT
p	ZONED DECIMAL (p=precision of value)
(p/2)+1	PACKED DECIMAL (p=precision of value)
x	FIXED LENGTH CHARACTER (x=length of string)
x	VARIABLE LENGTH CHARACTER (x=actual # of positions used)
3	TIME VALUE
4	DATE VALUE
10	TIMESTAMP VALUE

If you are performing this function on a calculated field, the result will be what is required to store the calculated value.

1. Assume that a field called CATDSC is defined as a fixed-length character field with a length of 40. In this case,

   `LENGTH(CATDSC)`

   will return a value of 40. If this field were defined as a variable-length field, the value returned would depend on what that field contained on any given record.

2. Assume that a field called CUST# is defined as a packed-decimal field with a length of 5 with 0 decimals. In this case,

   `LENGTH(CUST#)`

   will return a value of 3.

The LOCATE Function

The LOCATE function is used to search a string for a set of characters and to return the starting position of that string, if found. You can optionally specify a starting position at which the search is to begin. If the search string is not found, the value returned will be a zero. The syntax of the LOCATE function is

`LOCATE(search string, source string [,starting position])`

The result of this function is a large integer value.

For example,

1. Let's assume a field call ADDR is 30 bytes long and contains a value of "123 Main St.   ". The following

   `LOCATE('Main', ADDR)`

   will result in a value of 5.

The LTRIM Function

The LTRIM function removes leading blanks from a string value. This process is similar to the STRIP function using the LEADING option. The syntax of the LTRIM function is

`LTRIM(expression)`

The result of this function is a variable-length string. And if the expression contains a null value, the result will be a null value.

1. Let's assume a field call ADDR is 30 bytes long and contains a value of "   123 Main St.   ". In this case,

   `LTRIM(ADDR)`

   will result in a value of "123 Main St.   ".

The MAX Function

The MAX function returns the highest value encountered within the set of values provided. This function is valid for any data type; however, each argument must be of the same data type. The syntax of the MAX function is

```
MAX(expression, expression [,expression ...])
```

The length of the result will be based on the size of the largest argument in the list. Also, the result can only be a null value when every argument contains a null value.

1. Let's assume three numeric fields called NBR1, NBR2, and NBR3 contain the values 23, 34, and 45 respectively. In this case,

```
MAX(NBR1,NBR2,NBR3)
```

will return a value of 45. The order in which the fields are entered is not important.

The MICROSECOND Function

The MICROSECOND function returns the microsecond portion of a timestamp, a string representation of a timestamp, or a timestamp duration. The result will be an integer value. If the expression contains a null value, the result will be a null value. The syntax of the MICROSECOND function is

```
MICROSECOND(expression)
```

The value returned will be between 0 and 999999 when you use a timestamp value. If you use a timestamp duration, the result will be a value between -999999 and 999999.

1. Assume that a field called TIMSTP is defined as a timestamp field and contains the value 1999-08-14-13.23.45.070149. In this case,

```
MICROSECOND(TIMSTP)
```

will return a value of 070149.

2. Assume that two fields are defined as timestamp fields and are called SLDDTE and CATDTE. SLDDTE has a value of 1999-08-14-15.45.32.145245 and CATDTE has a value of 1999-01-01-16.33.24.432543. In this case,

```
MICROSECOND(SLDDTE-CATDTE)
```

will return a value of 712,702.

The MIN Function

The MIN function returns the smallest value encountered within the set of values provided. Each argument must be of a type comparable with the other. The syntax of the MIN function is

```
MIN(expression, expression [,expression ...])
```

The length of the result is based on the size of the smallest argument in the list. Also, the result will be a null value if any of the arguments contains a null value.

1. Assume three numeric fields called NBR1, NBR2, and NBR3 contain the values 23, 34, and 45 respectively. In this case,

```
MIN(NBR1,NBR2,NBR3)
```

will return a value of 23. The order in which the fields are entered is not important.

The MINUTE Function

The MINUTE function returns the minute portion of a time, timestamp, time duration, or timestamp duration. The result is an integer value. If the expression contains a null value, the result will be a null value. The syntax of the MINUTE function is

```
MINUTE(expression)
```

The value returned will be between 0 and 59 when you use a time or timestamp value. If you use a time or timestamp duration, the result will be a value between -99 and 99.

1. Assume that a field called MNTTIM is defined as a time field and contains a value of 13:23:45. In this case,

```
MINUTE(MNTTIM)
```

will return a value of 23.

2. Assume that two fields are defined as timestamp fields and are called SLDDTE and CATDTE. SLDDTE has a value of 1999-08-14-15.45.32.145245 and CATDTE has a value of 1999-01-01-16.33.24.432543. In this case,

```
MINUTE(SLDDTE-CATDTE)
```

will return a value of 12.

The MOD Function

The MOD function divides the first expression by the second and returns the remainder. The value of the second expression cannot be 0. The syntax of the MOD function is

```
MOD(expression, expression)
```

The type of numeric value returned depends on the types of numbers used in the expressions.

1. Assume that we have two fields: SHPQTY, with a value of 23, and AMOUNT, with a value of 435.77. In this case,

   ```
   MOD(AMOUNT,SHPQTY)
   ```

   will return a value of 21.77.

2. If AMOUNT has a value of 435.00,

   ```
   MOD(AMOUNT,SHPQTY)
   ```

   will return a value of 21.00.

The MONTH Function

The MONTH function returns the month portion of a date, timestamp, date duration, or timestamp duration. The result will be an integer value. If the expression contains a null value, the result will be a null value. The syntax of the MONTH function is

```
MONTH(expression)
```

When you use a date or timestamp, the value returned will be between 1 and 12. When you use a date duration or a timestamp duration, the result will be a value between -99 and 99.

1. Assume that a field called CATDTE is defined as a date field and contains a value of 1999-08-14. In this case,

   ```
   MONTH(CATDTE)
   ```

   will return a value of 08.

2. Assume that two fields are defined as timestamp fields and are called SLDDTE and CATDTE. SLDDTE has a value of 1999-08-14-15.45.32.145245 and CATDTE has a value of 1999-01-01-16.33.24.432543. In this case,

   ```
   MONTH(SLDDTE-CATDTE)
   ```

   will return a value of 7.

The NODENAME Function

The NODENAME function returns the database name of the system in which a particular row is located (see Chapter 9 for a discussion of distributive processing with SQL).

The NODENUMBER Function

The NODENUMBER function returns the number of the node in which a particular row is located (see Chapter 9 for a discussion of distributive processing with SQL).

The NOW Function

The NOW function returns the current timestamp based on the system where the application is running. Using this function is the same as using the CURTIME function or the special register CURRENT_TIMESTAMP. The syntax of the NOW function is

```
NOW()
```

This function does not have any arguments. However, you are required to specify the parentheses.

The NULLIF Function

The NULLIF function is used to return a null value when two expressions are equal. The syntax of the NULLIF function is

```
NULLIF(expression, expression)
```

When both parameters in the function are equal, a null value is returned. If the values are not equal, the value of the first parameter is returned.

The PARTITION Function

The PARTITION function returns the partition number of the row retrieved when you use the hashing function of the partitioning keys specified for the row (see Chapter 8 for a discussion of partitioning keys).

The POSITION or POSSTR Function

The POSITION or POSSTR function is similar to the LOCATE function in that the starting position of a search string is returned. The difference is that you cannot specify a starting position with these functions. The syntaxes of the POSITION and POSSTR functions are

```
POSITION(search string IN source string)
POSSTR(source string, search string)
```

The POWER Function

The POWER function raises a number to the power of another number. The result of this function is a double-precision, floating-point value. If either expression contains a null value, the result will be a null value. The syntax of the POWER function is

```
POWER(expression, expression)
```

1. Let's assume you have two fields called B and P, with B containing a value of 2 and P containing a value of 4. In this case,

```
POWER(B,P)
```

will result in a value of 16.

The QUARTER Function

The QUARTER function returns a value of 1 to 4 for a specified date. This value represents the quarter in which the date falls for the specific year. For example, a date in January will be in the first quarter, whereas a date in September will be in the third quarter. The syntax of the QUARTER function is

```
QUARTER(expression)
```

The value of the expression must be a date or a timestamp.

1. Let's assume that a date field called CATDTE has a value of 1996-10-20. In this case,

```
QUARTER(CATDTE)
```

will return a value of 4.

The REAL Function

The REAL function lets you convert a number or a character representation of a number into its single-precision floating-point equivalent. The syntax of the REAL function is

```
REAL(expression)
REAL(character expression)
```

The RRN Function

The RRN function returns the relative record of the row retrieved from the specified file. The syntax of the RRN function is

```
RRN(file name)
```

When you specify the file name, you cannot qualify the file name unless you are using SQL naming standards. If the file name specified is an SQL view, the value returned is the node number of the view's base table. If the view contains multiple files, the relative record number will be for the first file name on the outer select.

The result of this function is an integer value. The result can be a null value.

The RTRIM Function

The RTRIM function removes trailing blanks from a string value. This process is similar to the STRIP function using the TRAILING option. The syntax of the RTRIM function is

```
RTRIM(expression)
```

The result of this function is a variable-length string. If the expression contains a null value, the result will be a null value.

1. Let's assume a field called ADDR is 30 bytes long and contains a value of "123 Main St." In this case,

   ```
   RTRIM(ADDR)
   ```

   will result in a variable-length value of "123 Main St.".

The SECOND Function

The SECOND function returns the seconds portion of a time, timestamp, time duration, or timestamp duration. The result will be an integer value. If the expression contains a null value, the result will be a null value. The syntax of the SECOND function is

```
SECOND(expression)
```

The value returned will be between 0 and 59 when you use a time or timestamp value. If you use a time or timestamp duration, the result will be a value between -99 and 99.

1. Assume that a field called MNTTIM is defined as a time field and contains a value of 13:23:45. In this case,

   ```
   SECOND(MNTTIM)
   ```

   will return a value of 45.

2. Assume that two fields are defined as timestamp fields and are called SLDDTE and CATDTE. SLDDTE has a value of 1999-08-14-15.45.32.145245 and CATDTE has a value of 1999-01-01-16.33.24.432543. In this case,

   ```
   SECOND(SLDDTE-CATDTE)
   ```

   will return a value of 7.

The SMALLINT Function

The SMALLINT function lets you convert a number or a character representation of a number into its small integer equivalent. The syntax of the SMALLINT function is

```
SMALLINT(expression)
SMALLINT(character expression)
```

The SQRT Function

The SQRT function returns the square root of a number. The value of the expression must be greater than 0. The syntax of the SQRT function is

```
SQRT(expression)
```

The result of this function is always a double-precision, floating-point number. However, if the expression contains a null value, the result will be a null value.

1. Let's assume that a field called NUMBER contains a value of 10. In this case,

   `SQRT(NUMBER)`

   will return a value of 3.1622776601683795E+000.

2. If NUMBER contains a value of 225,

   `SQRT(NUMBER)`

   will return a value of 1.5000000000000000E+001.

The STRIP Function

The STRIP function takes a character value and converts it into a variable-length value. This is accomplished by either trailing or leading characters being removed from the character value. The syntax of the STRIP function is

```
STRIP(expression [[,BOTH | ,B] | [,LEADING | ,L] | [,TRAILING |
      ,T] [,strip character]])
```

The use of the BOTH, LEADING, or TRAILING arguments lets you strip a character either from the front, the back, or from both. Normally, the character stripped is a blank. But you can use any character value as the strip character. You must remember however, that the STRIP function is case-sensitive.

If you do not specify any values after the expression, the default is to strip leading and trailing blanks from the character string. If all characters are stripped from the string in the expression, the result is an empty variable-length string.

If the expression contains a field with a null value, the result will be a null value.

1. Let's assume a field called CATDSC contains a value of "   Description   " with three leading and five trailing blanks.

   `STRIP(CATDSC)`

   results in "Description".

   `STRIP(CATDSC,L)`

   results in "Description   ".

   `STRIP(CATDSC,T)`

   results in "   Description".

2. Now assume there are no trailing blanks in the field.

   `STRIP(CATDSC,T,'n')`

   results in "   Descriptio".

The SUBSTRING Function

The SUBSTRING or SUBSTR function lets you extract a portion of a string value. The result of the expression will be a character value. The following are samples of syntax for these functions:

```
SUBSTRING(expression, start, length) or

SUBSTR(expression, start, length) or

SUBSTRING(expression FROM start FOR length) or
```

You must be careful that the starting position and length specified do not exceed the actual length of the string. If this happens, the statement will fail. The SUBSTRING version of this function can be in two different forms, but they work exactly the same.

If you want to read a file with no external definition, you will use this function to extract the data into meaningful segments. However, because there are no functions that will convert a string value to a numeric value, you are limited in the type of processing you can perform.

1. Let's assume that a field called CATLG# contains a value of "A597-3996A". Either

```
SUBSTR(CATLG#,1,4)
```

or

```
SUBSTRING(CATLG# FROM 1 FOR 4)
```

will return a value of A597.

The TIME Function

The TIME function returns the time portion of a time, a timestamp, or a string representation of a time. The result will be a time value. The time value returned will be in the ISO format. The syntax of the TIME function is

```
TIME(expression)
```

If the expression contains a null value, the result will be a null value.

1. Assume that a field called MNTTIM is defined as a timestamp field and contains a value of 1999-08-14-13.23.45.658447. In this case,

```
TIME(MNTTIM)
```

will return a value of 13.23.45.

The TIMESTAMP Function

The TIMESTAMP function returns a timestamp from either a single value or from two values. The syntax of this function is

```
TIMESTAMP(expression [,expression])
```

When only one argument is used, the value must be a timestamp, a string representation of a timestamp, or a character string with a length of 14. When two arguments are used, the first argument must be a date or a string representation of a date and the second argument must be a time or a string representation of a time. The result is the combination of the two arguments. If the expression contains a null value, the result will be a null value.

A character string with a length of 14 refers to a string defined with the following form: *yyyyxxddhhmmss* where *yyyy* equals year, *xx* equals month, *dd* equals day, *hh* equals hour, *mm* equals minutes, and *ss* equals seconds. When you use this form, the timestamp will contain a microsecond value of 000000, because no microseconds are accounted for within this form. For example,

1. Let's assume that a field called MNTDTE is defined as a date field and has a value of 1999-08-14. Also, assume that a field called MNTTIM is defined as a time field with a value of 13:23:45. In this case,

```
TIMESTAMP(MNTDTE,MNTTIM)
```

will return a value of 1999-08-14-13.23.45.000000.

The TRANSLATE Function

The TRANSLATE function converts all lowercase characters in a string into their equivalent uppercase values or converts a string based on specific from and to values. The value of the expression must be a character value.

The syntax of this function is

```
TRANSLATE(expression [,to-string [,from-string
     [,pad character]]])
```

The first form of this function is very easy. If you specify only the string value, that string will be converted to uppercase. Using this form of the TRANSLATE function is the same as using the UCASE function.

In the second form, you are required to specify at least the from-string and to-string character changes. First, you specify what the new characters will be (to-string). Then you define which characters are to be changed (from-string).

You also can specify a *pad* character. You use the pad character to pad the to string with a character when the from string is longer than the to string.

1. Let's assume that a field called STRING contains a value of abc.

```
TRANSLATE(STRING)
```

will result in a value of ABC.

2. If STRING contains a value of ABc123deFGh, then

```
TRANSLATE(STRING)
```

will result in a value of ABC123DEFGH.

3. If STRING contains a value of Papa's Park Place Palace, then

```
TRANSLATE(STRING,'%%','PL')
```

will result in a value of %apa's %ark %%ace %a%ace.

The TRIM Function

The TRIM function is the same as the STRIP function except that the format is slightly different. The syntax of the TRIM function is

```
TRIM([[,BOTH | ,B] | [,LEADING | ,L] [,TRAILING | ,T]
[,strip character]]
FROM expression)
```

The FROM keyword is not required if you specify only a string value without any other values.

The TRIM function will result in a variable-length value, because either trailing or leading characters are removed from the character value.

The use of the BOTH, LEADING, or TRAILING arguments lets you strip a character either from the front, the back, or from both. Normally, the character stripped is a blank. However, you can use any character value as the strip character. You must remember, also, that the TRIM function is case-sensitive.

If you do not specify what characters are to be trimmed for the expression, the default strips both leading and trailing blanks from the character string. If all characters are stripped from the string in the expression, the result is an empty variable-length string.

If the expression contains a field with a null value, the result will be a null value.

1. Let's assume a field called CATDSC contains a value of "   Description   " with three leading and five trailing blanks.

   ```
   TRIM(CATDSC)
   ```

   results in "Description".

2. ```
   TRIM(LEADING FROM CATDSC)
   ```

   results in "Description   ".

3. ```
   TRIM(T FROM CATDSC)
   ```

   results in "   Description".

4. Now assume there are no trailing blanks in the field.

   ```
   STRIP(TRAILING 'n' FROM CATDSC)
   ```

   results in "   Descriptio".

The UCASE Function

The UCASE or UPPER function takes a string value and converts it to all uppercase values. These functions are the same as the TRANSLATE function when only one argument is provided. The syntax for these functions is

```
UCASE(expression) or UPPER(expression)
```

1. If you have a field called ADDR that contains a value of 123 Main St.,

```
UCASE(ADDR)
```

will return a value of 123 MAIN ST.

The VALUE Function

You use the VALUE function in conjunction with null values. This function returns the value of the first expression that is not a null value. The VALUE function is the same as the COALESE function. You are required to have at least two values specified in this function.

The syntax of the VALUE function is

```
VALUE(expression [,expression ...])
```

When a field contains a null value and is used in an arithmetic operation, the result is a null value. The VALUE function lets you override this feature. If all the expressions listed in this function are null values, the result is a null value.

Each expression used in the VALUE function must be of the same type. For example, if any expression is a date, every expression must be a date. If any expression is numeric, every expression must be numeric. The result of the function will be converted to the size of the maximum value contained within the function.

1. If you have a numeric field called FIELD and this field can contain null values, and you want to use this field in a calculation, you can enter the following function:

```
VALUE(FIELD, 0)
```

If the field contains a value, the value is returned first. If the field is null, the function returns a 0.

The VARCHAR Function

The VARCHAR function returns the variable-length equivalent of a character value, graphic, integer, decimal, or floating point value. The syntax of each VARCHAR function is

```
VARCHAR(character expression [, (length | DEFAULT) [,integer]])
VARCHAR(graphic expression [, (length | DEFAULT) [,integer]])
VARCHAR(integer expression)
VARCHAR(decimal expression [, decimal character])
VARCHAR(floating point expression [, decimal character])
```

The second argument of the character version of this function defines the length attribute of the variable length value created. Unless the value can be null, the length specified must be an integer value between 1 and 32740. If the value can be a null value, the valid range is between 1 and 32739.

If you don't specify the length or you specify DEFAULT, the length is calculated based on the type of string data contained in the expression (e.g., SBCS, mixed data; universal character set (UCS-2), graphic data).

You use the optional third argument to specify a valid CCSID value that represents the type of data being processed.

When specifying the graphic version of this function, you will specify either an expression that returns a GRAPHIC or VARGRAPHIC value. This value is then converted into its character equivalent. As with the character version, you can specify the length of the variable character.

When you specify the integer version of this function, you will specify an integer value. The result will be the varying character equivalent of the integer.

When you specify the decimal or floating-point version of this function, you will specify either a decimal or floating-point expression. Optionally, you can specify what character is to be used to represent the decimal point.

The VARGRAPHIC Function

The VARGRAPHIC function returns a graphic string representation of a character value. The syntax of this function is

```
VARGRAPHIC(expression [, (length | DEFAULT) [,integer]])
```

Use the second argument to define the length attribute of the variable length value created. Unless the value can be null, the length specified must be an integer value between 1 and 16370. If the value can be a null value, the valid range is between 1 and 16369.

If you don't specify the length or you specify DEFAULT, the length is calculated based on the length of the string value of the expression.

You use the optional third argument to specify a valid DBCS or UCS-2 CCSID.

The WEEK Function

The WEEK function returns an integer value that represents the relative week within a year for a date. The values returned will be from 1 to 53. The syntax of the WEEK function is

```
WEEK(expression)
```

The expression within this function must be either a date or a timestamp value. If the expression results in a null value, the result of this function will be a null value.

1. Let's assume a date field called CURDAT contains a value of 1999-09-15. In this case,

```
WEEK(CURDAT)
```

will return a value of 38, since the date is in the 38th week of the year.

The YEAR Function

The YEAR function returns the year portion of a date, timestamp, date duration, or timestamp duration. The result is an integer value. The year returned will always be a four-digit year, regardless of how the date field is defined. The syntax for the YEAR function is

```
YEAR(expression)
```

If the expression contains a null value, the result will be null. When you use a date or timestamp, the value returned will be between 1 and 9999. When you use a date duration or timestamp duration, the result will be a value between -9999 and 9999.

1. Assume that a field CATDTE is defined as a date field and contains a value of 1999-08-14. In this case,

   ```
   DAY(CATDTE)
   ```

   will return a value of 1999.

2. Assume that two fields, SLDDTE and CATDTE, are defined as timestamp fields. SLDDTE has a value of 1999-08-14-15.45.32.145245 and CATDTE has a value of 1999-01-01-16.33.24.432543. In this case,

   ```
   YEAR(SLDDTE-CATDTE)
   ```

   will return a value of 0.

The ZONED Function

The ZONED function returns the zoned-decimal representation of a number or a character string. You must provide the first argument; the remaining arguments are optional. The syntax of the ZONED function is

```
ZONED(expression [,precision [,scale]])
ZONED(character expression [,precision [,scale]])
```

The second argument represents the precision or size of the returned value (between 1 and 31). If you do not specify this argument, a default value will be used (15 for floating-point, decimal, numeric, or non-zero scale binary; 11 for large integer; and 5 for small integer).

The third argument specifies the scale or number of decimal positions in the returned value. If you do not specify this argument, a default of 0 is used. For example,

1. Let's assume that a field called NUMBER contains a value of 9.6734. In this case,

   ```
   ZONED(NUMBER)
   ```

will return a value of 9.

2. In a field with the same value as above,

```
ZONED(NUMBER,5,2)
```

will return a value of 9.67.

3.   `ZONED('123.45',5,2)`

will return a value of 123.45.

TRIGONOMETRIC FUNCTIONS

In addition to the scalar functions we have discussed so far, SQL provides a number of trigonometric and geometric scalar functions (see Table 4.3). You won't need these functions for most business programming, so we won't go into detail here. For more information about these functions, refer to the IBM documentation for SQL.

TABLE 4.3
Trigonometric and Geometric Scalar Functions

ACOS	Returns the arc cosine of a number
ANTILOG	Returns the anti-logarithm (base 10) of a number
ASIN	Returns the arc sine of a number
ATAN	Returns the arc tangent of a number
ATANH	Returns the hyperbolic arc tangent of a number
COS	Returns the cosine of a number
COSH	Returns the hyperbolic cosine of a number
COT	Returns the cotangent of a number
DEGREES	Returns the number of degrees in an angle
EXP	Takes the value of the natural logarithm (e) and raises it to the power specified in the expression
LN	Returns the natural logarithm of a number
LOG or LOG10	Returns the common logarithm (base 10) of a number
SIN	Returns the sine of a number
SINH	Returns the hyperbolic sine of a number
TAN	Returns the tangent of a number
TANH	Returns the hyperbolic tangent of a number

BIT COMPARISON FUNCTIONS

SQL also provides a number of bit comparison functions in addition to all the other scalar functions we have discussed (see Table 4.4). For more information about these functions, refer to the IBM documentation for SQL.

TABLE 4.4
Bit Comparison Functions

LAND	Performs a logical AND operation against a specified number of string values and returns the results
LNOT	Performs a logical NOT operation against a string value and returns the results
LOR	Performs a logical OR operation against a specified number of string values and returns the results
XOR	Performs a logical XOR operation against a specified number of string values and returns the result

SPECIAL REGISTERS

Besides the above scalar functions, SQL provides some special registers that you can use to obtain static information. You cannot change the values of special registers; their purpose is only to provide information.

The USER Register

The USER register identifies the user profile of the person currently executing the application. The result is a variable character field with a length of 18.

The CURRENT DATE Register

The CURRENT DATE (or CURRENT_DATE) register provides the current date of the system where the application is executing. The format of the date returned is based on the environment in which the statement is executing.

The CURRENT SERVER Register

The CURRENT SERVER (or CURRENT_SERVER) register provides the ID of the relational database to which you are currently connected. If your local database is not in the relational database directory, you are not allowed to use this register. The value returned will be defined as a variable character with a length of 18.

The CURRENT TIME Register

The CURRENT TIME (or CURRENT_TIME) register provides the current time of the system where the application is executing. The format of the time returned is dependent upon the environment where the application is being executed.

The CURRENT TIMESTAMP Register

The CURRENT TIMESTAMP (or CURRENT_TIMESTAMP) register provides the current timestamp value of the system where the application is executing.

The CURRENT TIMEZONE Register

The CURRENT TIMEZONE (or CURRENT_TIMEZONE) register provides the difference between the current time and the Universal Coordinated Time (Greenwich Mean Time). The difference is presented as a time duration with the first two digits representing the hours, the next two digits representing the minutes, and the last two digits representing the seconds. The hours will be a value anywhere between 0 and 24. For this register to provide a meaningful value, the system value QUTCOFFSET value must be set correctly.

DATA EXAMPLES

Now let's look at some actual data examples using several of the scalar functions we have discussed. The examples we present here use the sample database in Appendix A to help show the effect each function has against actual data. These examples also demonstrate how you can mix and match the functions.

1. Assume we use the following statement:

```
SELECT CATLG#,CPRICE,
       DECIMAL(DECIMAL(CPRICE*1.03+.99,7,0)-.01,7,2)
       AS "New Price"
  FROM CATALOG
```

This statement will list the catalog number, current price, and the calculated price for every record in the catalog master file. The calculated price is based on a 3 percent increase, rounding to the next highest dollar value and then subtracting one cent. This statement produces the results presented in Table 4.5.

TABLE 4.5
Results of the Select Statement in Example 1

CATLG#	CPRICE	New Price
A597-3996A	59.99	61.99
A225-8037A	65.00	66.99
B115-3170A	22.00	22.99
B501-1218D	15.00	15.99
C689-1192D	16.00	16.99
D805-0271C	32.99	33.99
C871-1139C	45.99	47.99
A658-4077A	130.95	134.99
A483-7921B	15.99	16.99
B489-7920B	15.99	16.99
B156-3780A	99.99	102.99
D362-7997A	135.00	139.99

2. Now assume we use the following statement:

```
SELECT CATLG#,CATDSC
  FROM CATALOG
 WHERE CTGRY# = 15
   AND SUBSTR(CATLG#,1,1) = 'B'
    OR CURYR$>3000
```

This statement selects items in the catalog master file where the category number is equal to 15 and the first character of the catalog number is a B or the current year sales is greater than $3000.00. This statement produces the results presented in Table 4.6.

TABLE 4.6
Results of the Select Statement in Example 2

CATLG#	CATDSC
A225-8037A	Pocket Size Cassette Player
B501-1218D	Solid Leotard - Blue
B156-3780A	Arctic Circle Mummy Sleeping Bag

3. If you want to list every item in the catalog master file that was entered after 1990, you could enter the following statement:

```
SELECT CATLG#,CATDSC
  FROM CATALOG
 WHERE SUBSTR(DIGITS(CATDTE),5,2) > '90'
```

In this example, the date had to be converted into a character value to extract the year portion because the date is in a month/day/year format. This statement produces the results presented in Table 4.7.

TABLE 4.7
Results of the Select Statement in Example 3

CATLG#	CATDSC
A483-7921B	Case 10W40 Motor Oil
B489-7920B	Case 10W30 Motor Oil
B156-3780A	Arctic Circle Mummy Sleeping Bag
D362-7997A	Portable CD Player

4. Assume that the catalog description field in the catalog master file is a variable-length field. If you want to see the last five characters of the description field, you can enter the following statement:

```
SELECT CATLG#,SUBSTR(CATDSC,LENGTH(CATDSC)-4,5)
                AS "Last 5 Char"
  FROM CATALOG
```

This statement produces the results presented in Table 4.8.

TABLE 4.8

Results of the Select Statement in Example 4

CATLG#	Last 5 Char
A597-3996A	g Bag
A225-8037A	layer
B115-3170A	klace
B501-1218D	Blue
C689-1192D	Green
D805-0271C	Chair
C871-1139C	Chair
A658-4077A	Tent
A483-7921B	r Oil
B489-7920B	r Oil
B156-3780A	g Bag
D362-7997A	layer

5. If you want to execute the last example, but the field is a fixed-length field, you can still do so using the STRIP function. Here's a statement you can use:

```
SELECT CATLG#,SUBSTR(STRIP(CATDSC),
            LENGTH(STRIP(CATDSC))-4,5) AS "Last 5 Char"
  FROM CATALOG
```

This statement produces the results presented in Table 4.9.

TABLE 4.9

Results of the Statement in Example 5

CATLG#	Last 5 Char
A597-3996A	g Bag
A225-8037A	layer
B115-3170A	klace
B501-1218D	Blue
C689-1192D	Green
D805-0271C	Chair
C871-1139C	Chair
A658-4077A	Tent
A483-7921B	r Oil
B489-7920B	r Oil
B156-3780A	g Bag
D362-7997A	layer

6. Finally, if you want to find every record in the catalog master file that contains the letters b, a, and g regardless of capitalization, you can use the following statement:

```
SELECT CATLG#, CATDSC
  FROM CATALOG
 WHERE TRANSLATE(CATDSC) LIKE '%BAG%'
```

This statement produces the results in Table 4.10.

TABLE 4.10

Results of the Statement in Example 6

CATLG#	CATDSC
A597-3996A	Sahara Desert Mummy Sleeping Bag
D805-0271C	Vinyl Bean Bag Chair
C871-1139C	Corduroy Bean Bag Chair
B156-3780A	Arctic Circle Mummy Sleeping Bag

Chapter 5

Data Summarization

Up to this point, we have been discussing the selection and processing of detail information from a file. With SQL, you also can extract summary information from a file. Column functions, together with three clauses within the SELECT statement, provide the mechanism for summarizing data.

COLUMN FUNCTIONS

Column functions perform an operation over many records in a file and return a single value for a group of records. This process is the same as that of a group summary operation.

Column functions are actually very straightforward and do not require a lot of explanation. Column functions are only allowed within the SELECT statement; they not available for the other data-manipulation-language statements.

Column functions are different from scalar functions in that you cannot embed column functions within each other. You can, however, embed scalar functions within a column function. This capability can be useful for controlling the size of the value presented in the resulting table of a summarized operation.

When you specify a column function, at least one valid field name must exist within the function. We discuss the available column functions in the following sections.

The AVG Function

The AVG function returns the average value of the specified expression. This function is valid only for numeric fields. The syntax of this function is

```
AVG([ALL | DISTINCT] expression)
```

The number of decimal positions in the result of the AVG function is determined by the size and type of the numeric fields used in the expression.

When a record is processed by the AVG function and the value of the expression for that record results in a null value, the AVG function will ignore that record. This means that although the SELECT statement may process the record, that record will not be figured into the result of the AVG function. Therefore, you may have 10 records that were processed but the average may be based on only 9 records because of null values.

The DISTINCT argument indicates that only unique values within the group are to be averaged. If two or more records have the same value, only one will be considered. Records that are excluded will not be considered when the average is calculated. If every record processed contains a null value, the result of the AVG function will be a null value.

1. This function returns the average of the field called CURYR$ for each group selected:

   `AVG(CURYR$)`

2. This function returns the average of the sum of the fields CURYR$ and YR1$ for each group selected:

   `AVG(CURYR$+YR1$)`

The COUNT Function

The COUNT function returns the number of records found within a group. The result is a number and will not contain a null value. If no records were processed, the result will be 0. The syntax of the COUNT function is

   `COUNT([* | [ALL | DISTINCT] expression])`

If you specify the "*" argument or the "ALL expression" arguments, every record within the group will be counted. If you use the DISTINCT argument, only those records with unique values for the expression will be counted.

1. This function returns the total number of records processed for each group selected.

   `COUNT(*)`

The MAX Function

The MAX function returns the maximum value encountered for a group of records. You can perform this function on numeric, character, or date values. When a character field is being processed, the result cannot exceed 256 characters. The syntax of the MAX function is

   `MAX([ALL | DISTINCT] expression)`

The DISTINCT argument does not have any effect on this column function; therefore, we recommend that you do not use this argument.

If the expression results in a null value and every record processed for a group is a null value, the result is a null value. Otherwise, the largest non-null value is returned.

1. This function returns the largest value found for a field called AMOUNT for each group selected.

   `MAX(AMOUNT)`

2. Now assume that a field called CATDTE is a numeric field with six digits and 0 decimals and that this field contains a date in *mm/dd/yy* format. If

you want to find the last year encountered for a group of records, you can use the following function:

```
MAX(SUBSTR(DIGITS(CATDTE),5,2)
```

The MIN Function

The MIN function returns the minimum value found for a group of records. You can perform this function on numeric, character, or date values. When a character field is processed, the result of the MIN function cannot exceed 256 characters. The syntax of the MIN function is

```
MIN([ALL | DISTINCT] expression)
```

The DISTINCT argument does not have any effect on this column function; therefore, we recommend that you do not use this argument.

If the expression results in a null value and every record processed for a group is a null value, the result is a null value. Otherwise, the smallest non-null value is returned.

1. This function returns the smallest value found for a field called AMOUNT for each group selected.

```
MIN(AMOUNT)
```

2. Now assume that a field called CATDTE is a numeric field with six digits and 0 decimals and that this field contains a date in *mm/dd/yy* format. If you want to find the earliest year encountered for a group of records, you can use the following function:

```
MIN(SUBSTR(DIGITS(CATDTE),5,2)
```

The STDDEV Function

The STDDEV function returns the standard deviation for an expression for a specific group of records. The expression must be a numeric value. Finding the standard deviation is the same as taking the square root of the variance for a group of records (see the VAR column function). The syntax of the STDDEV function is

```
STDDEV([ALL | DISTINCT] expression)
```

The result of this function is always a double-precision, floating-point value. The result can be a null value if this function is applied to any empty set of values (i.e., no records).

The DISTINCT argument indicates that only unique values within the group are to be used to calculate the standard deviation. If two or more records have the same value, only one will be considered.

1. If you want the standard deviation for a group of records over a numeric field called AMOUNT, you can enter the following function:

```
STDDEV(AMOUNT)
```

The SUM Function

The SUM function returns the total value for a group of records. This function is valid only for numeric fields. The syntax of this function is

```
SUM([ALL | DISTINCT] expression
```

If the result of the expression within the function is a null value, the null value will be ignored. Unlike the AVG function, ignoring null values won't affect summarization unless every record processed contains a null value. In that case, the result of the SUM function will be a null value.

The DISTINCT argument indicates that only unique values within the group are to be totaled. If two or more records have the same value, only one will be considered.

1. This function returns the total of the field called CURYR$ for each group selected.

```
SUM(CURYR$)
```

2. This function returns the total of the sum of the fields called CURYR$ and YR1$ for each group selected.

```
SUM(CURYR$+YR1$)
```

The VAR or VARIANCE Function

The VAR or VARIANCE function returns the variance for an expression for a specific group of records. The expression must be a numeric value. The syntax of this function is

```
VAR([ALL | DISTINCT] expression) or
VARIANCE([ALL | DISTINCT] expression)
```

Variance is calculated using the following formula:

```
SUM(X**2)/COUNT(X) - (SUM(X)/COUNT(X))**2
```

The result of this function is always a double-precision, floating-point value. The result can be a null value if you apply this function to any empty set of values (i.e., no records).

The DISTINCT argument indicates that only unique values within the group are to be used to calculate the variance. If two or more records have the same value, only one will be considered.

1. If you want the variance for a group of records over a numeric field called AMOUNT, enter

```
VAR(AMOUNT)
```

THE SELECT STATEMENT

Now that we have presented the column functions, you need to know how they are used within the SELECT statement. When you use column functions, three clauses are involved: the SELECT, GROUP BY, and HAVING clauses.

To specify data summarization, you must put at least one column function within the SELECT clause. This causes SQL to present only summarized information.

When you perform summary operations, you can still perform detail record selection. In this case, the record is tested first to see whether the conditions are true. Then and only then is that record included in the summary operation.

You can summarize the entire file and retrieve a single result, or you can summarize by specific fields. Summarizing by specific fields is the same as processing level breaks or intermediate summary totals. The one thing you cannot do is provide for intermediate totals and at the same time extract grand totals within the same SELECT statement.

Let's look now at how we can summarize data using the three clauses. The examples in this section show the results of the data summarization requests executed over the sample database provided in Appendix A.

The SELECT Clause

You use the SELECT clause to specify which data-summarization operations are to be performed. At least one column function is required in this clause to initiate data summarization.

If you specify only column functions in the select clause, you will receive one record that contains the totals requested. (This is the same as specifying that you want grand totals only.) In this case, no database fields will be specified outside of the column functions. However, constants are allowed within the SELECT clause, even when you are using column functions.

If you want to specify some type of intermediate summary operation against specific fields in your database, you place the database field names for which summarization is requested ahead of the column functions specified. When you do this, you also must specify those same database field names within the GROUP BY clause.

1. Let's say you want to provide the grand total of last year's sales from the catalog master file. To do so, you can enter the following statement:

```
SELECT SUM(YR1$) AS "Total Last Year Sales"
   FROM CATALOG
```

This statement produces the following results:

Total Last Year Sales

68761.42

2. Now let's say you want to see the total of last year's sales from the catalog master file for category 15 only. To do this, you can enter the following statement:

```
SELECT SUM(YR1$) AS "Total Sales for Catalog #15"
  FROM CATALOG
 WHERE CTGRY# = 15
```

This statement produces the following results:

Total Sales for Catalog #15
16053.28

The GROUP BY Clause

If you want to perform summary operations on a specific field or fields, you will use a combination of the SELECT and GROUP BY clauses. The syntax of the GROUP BY clause is

```
GROUP BY field name [,field name,...]
```

You place the fields you want to list in your resulting table (those not included in a column function) in the SELECT clause, then you specify those same field names in the GROUP BY clause. This is necessary because the GROUP BY clause, not the SELECT clause, is the mechanism that causes summary breaks.

The GROUP BY clause produces the resulting table by grouping records according to the fields specified in this clause. To be able to use the GROUP BY clause, a column function must be present in the SELECT clause. Also, commas must separate the field names.

An important point to remember is that any fields you specify in the SELECT clause that are not part of a column function must be specified here. Not specifying these fields is one of the most common mistakes you can make when you code a SELECT statement with column functions.

You can specify field names in the GROUP BY clause that are not in the SELECT clause, but you must use caution when you do this because the field names listed in the GROUP BY clause are not presented in the resulting table. In other words, only those fields in the SELECT clause are listed. GROUP BY fields provide the mechanism that causes level breaks for the column functions. Normally, any of the GROUP BY fields are the same ones in the SELECT clause.

The GROUP BY clause does not allow scalar functions, column functions, or arithmetic operations.

1. If you want to know the total current-year sales for each category within the catalog master file, you can enter the following statement:

```
SELECT CTGRY#, SUM(CURYR$) AS "Total Current Year Sales"
  FROM CATALOG
 GROUP BY CTGRY#
```

This statement produces the results listed in Table 5.1.

TABLE **5.1**
Results of the SELECT Statement in Example 1

CTGRY#	Total Current Year Sales
15	4963.95
24	4300.00
38	1056.00
64	6150.00
156	3260.17
348	2318.55

2. The following statement provides the total amount sold for each catalog number within the sales history file. However, this example shows what happens if you perform some type of scalar function on the SELECT clause. In this case, only the first four characters of the catalog number are being listed.

```
SELECT SUBSTR(CATLG#,1,4), SUM(AMOUNT) AS "Total Amount"
   FROM SALESHST
   GROUP BY CATLG#
```

This statement produces the results listed in Table 5.2.

TABLE **5.2**
Results of the SELECT Statement in Example 2

CATLG#	Total Amount
A225	41937.00
A483	3629.35
A597	2915.48
A658	14117.60
B115	4505.00
B156	7413.40
B489	4516.70
B501	14725.00
C689	12808.00
C871	5569.77
D362	270.00
D805	5223.26

As you can see, this probably would not be a meaningful extraction of data.

3. The following statement is not correct because it contains a calculated field within the GROUP BY clause:

```
SELECT CATLG#, SUM(AMOUNT)
  FROM SALESHST
  GROUP BY SUM(AMOUNT),CATLG#
```

The HAVING Clause

At times you may want to present a summarized total only when the results meet some type of condition. The HAVING clause lets you do this. The syntax of this clause is

```
HAVING predicate
```

The HAVING clause produces a resulting table by applying conditional tests to each group record produced by a column function. This clause functions similarly to the WHERE clause. What you need to remember is that the WHERE clause chooses records and the HAVING clause chooses groups.

To use the HAVING clause, there must be a column function in the SELECT clause. The group record will be provided only if the HAVING condition is true. Note that you are not required to use the GROUP BY clause when you use the HAVING clause, but you normally will.

When specifying the test conditions, you must use a column function in the HAVING clause. The column function you specify can be for any field in the file — it does not necessarily have to be the same as what is specified in the SELECT clause. One thing to remember is that you cannot condition a group by testing non-column function fields.

The same rules and operators available for the WHERE clause are available for the HAVING clause.

1. Let's say you want to list the total current-year sales for each category in the catalog master file, but you want to list only those categories that had a total sales greater than $3,000. You can use the following statement to accomplish this:

```
SELECT CTGRY#, SUM(CURYR$) AS "Total Sales"
  FROM CATALOG
  GROUP BY CTGRY#
HAVING SUM(CURYR$)>3000
```

This statement produces the results listed in Table 5.3.

TABLE 5.3
Results of the SELECT Statement in Example 1

CTGRY#	Total Sales
15	4963.95
24	4300.00
64	6150.00
156	3260.17

2. If you want the total current-year sales in the catalog master file for categories 15, 38, and 64, but you want only those with total sales greater than $3,000, you can enter the following statement:

```
SELECT CTGRY#, SUM(CURYR$) AS "Total Sales"
  FROM CATALOG
 WHERE CTGRY# IN(15,38,64)
 GROUP BY CTGRY#
HAVING SUM(CURYR$)>3000
```

This statement produces the results listed in Table 5.4.

TABLE 5.4
Results of the SELECT Statement in Example 2

CTGRY#	Total Sales
15	4963.95
64	6150.00

EXAMPLES

Now that we have explained the basic concepts involved in data summarization, here are some additional examples using the various column functions that are available. These examples show how you can mix and match the given functions.

1. If you want to know how many items are in category 15 within the catalog master file, you can enter the following statement:

```
SELECT COUNT(*)
  FROM CATALOG
 WHERE CTGRY# = 15
```

This statement produces the following results:

COUNT(*)
3

2. The following statement lists the total number of records, the total of the current-year sales, the average of the current-year sales, the lowest current-year sales figure, and the highest current-year sales figure in the catalog master file:

```
SELECT COUNT(*) AS "Count",
       SUM(CURYR$) AS "Total$",
       AVG(CURYR$) AS "Avg$",
       MIN(CURYR$) AS "Min$",
       MAX(CURYR$) AS "Max$",
       STDDEV(CURYR$) AS "Std Dev$",
       VAR(CURYR$) AS "Var$"
   FROM CATALOG
```

This statement produces the following results:

Count	Total$	Avg$	Min$	Max$	Std Dev$	Var$
12	21994.67	1832.8891	0.00	4030.00	1.2129856394482333E+003	1.4713341615076396E+006

3. The following statement lists the current-year sales divided by the number of records in the catalog master file. This is the same as saying AVG(CURYR$), except that the number of decimals in the result would be fewer with that statement.

```
SELECT SUM(CURYR$)/COUNT(*) AS "Average $ Per Sale"
   FROM CATALOG
```

This statement produces the following results:

Average $ Per Sale
1832.88

4. If you want to know how much a 10 percent increase in last year's sales would be, you can enter the following statement:

```
SELECT DECIMAL(SUM(YR1$)*1.10,9,2)
          AS "10% Increase Over Last Year"
   FROM CATALOG
```

This statement produces the following results:

10% Increase Over Last Year
75637.56

Chapter 6

Joining Files

When you process a SELECT statement, you are not limited to processing a single file; you can also join files to extract and process information. All the functions and tasks we have described so far are valid even when files are joined.

After we look at joining files, we examine the UNION clause, which provides a way to join the results of multiple SELECT statements.

JOINING FILES

Files can be joined in two ways — with the FROM clause using the JOIN subclause, or with the WHERE clause.

When we discuss joining files, we need to define four different types of joins. These are

Inner join — An inner join links records from two tables. Only records that match the testing will be included. Use of the WHERE clause results in an inner join.

Left outer join — A left outer join links records from two tables. However, if a record exists in the first table that cannot be matched with the second table, that record will be included in the resulting table with the records that can be matched.

Exception join — With an exception join, only the records in the first table that cannot be matched with the second table will be included in the resulting table.

Cross join — A cross join links every record in the first table with every record in the second table. The result is known as a *Cartesian Product*.

The FROM Clause

When you want to join several files together, you must tell SQL which files are to be joined and what kind of join you want to perform. You can do this with the FROM clause's JOIN subclause or within the WHERE clause. The format of the FROM clause is

```
FROM <library/>file name [AS] [alias]
     [ [INNER | LEFT OUTER | EXCEPTION] JOIN file name ON
          field name = field name
          [AND field name = field name ...] | CROSS JOIN file
name], ...
```

You can join up to 32 files, although for performance reasons you generally should not join more than seven or eight files. Commas must separate the files. You can also join a file to itself.

When you join files together, you are not required to have a one-to-one relationship between the files. For example, joining three files in a one-many-many relationship is a valid combination.

You specify the linking of files within the JOIN subclause using the ON keyword. You specify one field name from the first table and compare that field to another field in the second table. If you have more than one set of fields to compare, you specify the AND keyword between the sets of fields.

If you do not specify the ON keyword within the JOIN subclause, you will receive a cross join. In this case, the resulting table will contain every possible combination of records. In other words, each record in the first file will be joined with every record in the second file. If one file contains 2,000 records and the other 6,000 records, the resulting table will contain 12,000,000 records! So you definitely want to be careful with this type of join.

One common mistake is to use equal and not-equal conditioning when you are joining files. Not-equal conditions do not provide the mechanism for determining whether a record is not in another file. Most often, you use the equal sign when you are specifying joining conditions. If you need to know when a record is not in another file, use either the EXCEPTION JOIN or a subselect (see Chapter 7).

If any of the joined files have fields with the same name and you want to use those fields, you must qualify the field names with the name of the file from which the data is to be retrieved. This is true no matter where the field name is used. To qualify the field, you use the file name, a period, and then the field name (e.g., CATALOG.CTGRY).

To avoid having to key the file name each time, you can use a correlated name or alias for each file. The syntax for specifying a correlated name is the file name and the correlated name, separated by a space (e.g., CUSTFILE F1). The maximum length of a correlated name is 10 characters. Optionally, you can specify the AS subclause before you specify the correlated name.

If you use the LEFT OUTER JOIN function, any fields referenced in the SELECT clause that come from the second file will contain their default values when no match can be made with the record in the first file.

One last point about joining files together: Depending on which files you use and how you link them, you may end up with a sorted table because SQL tries to optimize how to link the files and may use a different path than the one you anticipated. If the resulting table needs to be in any particular sort sequence, you should use the ORDER BY clause to ensure proper sorting.

The WHERE Clause

You can use the WHERE clause to specify how to join files together. To accomplish this, you compare fields from one database file to those of another. SQL provides the links necessary to accomplish the join operation, so you must be careful how you join files together. If you do not specify the proper testing conditions, you will get erroneous results. Generally, you join files together by means of equal tests, but you are not limited to this approach.

The syntax of the WHERE clause is

```
WHERE predicate
```

The following examples demonstrate how to join files together with the JOIN and the WHERE clauses.

1. Let's say you want to list each item in the catalog master file and the category description for each item. You can do this by joining the catalog and category master files together. In this case, the join is a one-to-one relationship. To do this join, you can use the following statement:

```
SELECT CATLG#,CATALOG.CTGRY#,CTDESC
  FROM CATALOG INNER JOIN CATEGORY
    ON CATALOG.CTGRY# = CATEGORY.CTGRY#

SELECT CATLG#,CATALOG.CTGRY#,CTDESC
  FROM CATALOG, CATEGORY
 WHERE CATALOG.CTGRY# = CATEGORY.CTGRY#
```

In this example, notice the qualification of the category number field, required because both files contain the same name and SQL needs to know from which file to extract the data. The above statement produces the results in Table 6.1.

TABLE 6.1
Results of the SELECT Statement in Example 1

CATLG#	CTGRY#	CTDESC
A597-3996A	15	Sporting Goods
A658-4077A	15	Sporting Goods
B156-3780A	15	Sporting Goods
A225-8037A	24	Home Electronics
D362-7997A	24	Home Electronics
B115-3170A	38	Jewelry
B501-1218D	64	Women's Apparel
C689-1192D	64	Women's Apparel
C871-1139C	156	Furniture & Accessories
D805-0271C	156	Furniture & Accessories
A483-7921B	348	Auto Supplies
B489-7920B	348	Auto Supplies

2. In this example we use a correlated name instead of the file names. As you can see, this statement is much easier to work with.

```
SELECT CATLG#,A.CTGRY#,CTDESC
  FROM CATALOG A INNER JOIN CATEGORY B
    ON A.CTGRY# = B.CTGRY#

SELECT CATLG#,A.CTGRY#,CTDESC
  FROM CATALOG A, CATEGORY B
WHERE A.CTGRY# = B.CTGRY#
```

3. The following statement links each record in the order header file to each record in the order item file where the order numbers are the same. This is a one-to-many relationship. Only the order number field is qualified because it is the only used field common to both files.

```
SELECT A.ORDER#,CUST#,CATLG#,ORDQTY
  FROM ORDERHDR A INNER JOIN ORDERITM B
    ON A.ORDER# = B.ORDER#

SELECT A.ORDER#,CUST#,CATLG#,ORDQTY
  FROM ORDERHDR A, ORDERITM B
WHERE A.ORDER# = B.ORDER#
```

This statement produces the results in Table 6.2.

TABLE 6.2
Results of the SELECT Statement in Example 3

ORDER#	CUST#	CATLG#	ORDQTY
1034	32418	A597-3996A	50
1069	62990	B501-1218D	380
1069	62990	C689-1192D	100
1108	411	A225-8037A	189
1187	392	B115-3170A	79
1212	8395	C689-1192D	100
1226	392	C871-1139C	10
1226	392	D805-0271C	8
1227	62990	B501-1218D	300
1228	32418	A658-4077A	5
1246	32418	A658-4077A	88
1259	411	A225-8037A	100
1259	411	B156-3780A	50
1259	411	C871-1139C	80
1272	1583	B489-7920B	250

continued

TABLE **6.2** CONTINUED

ORDER#	CUST#	CATLG#	ORDQTY
1273	62990	B501-1218D	100
1273	62990	C689-1192D	488
1314	392	D805-0271C	60
1316	392	B115-3170A	8
1328	392	A225-8037A	300
1360	32418	A597-3996A	2
1362	1583	A483-7921B	200
1362	1583	B489-7920B	80
1365	8395	B115-3170A	89
1375	411	B115-3170A	50
1375	411	D805-0271C	20
1400	411	A225-8037A	18
1401	62990	C689-1192D	150
1410	8395	D362-7997A	2
1410	8395	D805-0271C	60
1420	392	A225-8037A	44
1420	392	D805-0271C	7
1423	32418	A658-4077A	7
1423	32418	B156-3780A	60
1469	1583	A483-7921B	130
1470	32418	A658-4077A	8
1483	411	C871-1139C	36
1492	62990	B501-1218D	300

4. The following statement links each record in the order header file to each record in the order item file where the order numbers are NOT the same. This statement is unlikely to produce a desirable result because the order headers will be joined with unrelated item records.

```
SELECT A.ORDER#,CUST#,CATLG#,ORDQTY
  FROM ORDERHDR A INNER JOIN ORDERITM B
    ON A.ORDER# <> B.ORDER#

SELECT A.ORDER#,CUST#,CATLG#,ORDQTY
  FROM ORDERHDR A, ORDERITM B
 WHERE A.ORDER# <> B.ORDER#
```

This statement produces the results in Table 6.3.

TABLE 6.3
Results of the SELECT Statement in Example 4

ORDER#	CUST#	CATLG#	ORDQTY	Actual Order Joined
1034	32418	B501-1218D	380	1069
1034	32418	C689-1192D	100	1069
1034	32418	A225-8037A	189	1108
1034	32418	B115-3170A	79	1187
1034	32418	C689-1192D	100	1212
.	.	.	.	.
.	.	.	.	.
.	.	.	.	.
1069	62990	A597-3996A	50	1034
1069	62990	A225-8037A	189	1108
1069	62990	B115-3170A	79	1187
1069	62990	C689-1192D	100	1212
1069	62990	C871-1139C	10	1226
.	.	.	.	.
.	.	.	.	.
.	.	.	.	.

(*Table 6.3 contains 1026 records.*)

5. If you want to know which records exist in the order header that are not in the order item file (an exception join), you can use the following statement:

```
SELECT A.ORDER#,CUST#
  FROM ORDERHDR A EXCEPTION JOIN ORDERITM B
    ON A.ORDER# = B.ORDER#
```

This statement produces the following results:

ORDER#	CUST#
1411	411

6. The following statement links each record in the order header file to each record in the order item file. However, if any records do not exist in the order item for the order header, the order header data will still be shown. This type of request is not possible using the WHERE clause.

```
SELECT A.ORDER#,CUST#,CATLG#,ORDQTY
  FROM ORDERHDR A LEFT OUTER JOIN ORDERITM B
    ON A.ORDER# = B.ORDER#
```

This statement produces the results in Table 6.4.

TABLE 6.4

Results of the SELECT Statement in Example 6

ORDER#	CUST#	CATLG#	ORDQTY
1034	32418	A597-3996A	50
1069	62990	B501-1218D	380
1069	62990	C689-1192D	100
1108	411	A225-8037A	189
1187	392	B115-3170A	79
1212	8395	C689-1192D	100
1226	392	C871-1139C	10
1226	392	D805-0271C	8
1227	62990	B501-1218D	300
1228	32418	A658-4077A	5
1246	32418	A658-4077A	88
1259	411	A225-8037A	100
1259	411	B156-3780A	50
1259	411	C871-1139C	80
1272	1583	B489-7920B	250
1273	62990	B501-1218D	100
1273	62990	C689-1192D	488
1314	392	D805-0271C	60
1316	392	B115-3170A	8
1328	392	A225-8037A	300
1360	32418	A597-3996A	2
1362	1583	A483-7921B	200
1362	1583	B489-7920B	80
1365	8395	B115-3170A	89
1375	411	B115-3170A	50
1375	411	D805-0271C	20
1400	411	A225-8037A	18
1401	62990	C689-1192D	150
1410	8395	D362-7997A	2
1410	8395	D805-0271C	60
1411	411		0
1420	392	A225-8037A	44
1420	392	D805-0271C	7
1423	32418	A658-4077A	7
1423	32418	B156-3780A	60
1469	1583	A483-7921B	130
1470	32418	A658-4077A	8
1483	411	C871-1139C	36
1492	62990	B501-1218D	300

7. The following statement lists every record that has a substitute catalog number and its description, together with the description of the substitute number. Because this file is joined to itself, you must use field qualifications and correlated names.

```
SELECT A.CATLG#,A.CATDSC,A.SUB#,B.CATDSC
  FROM CATALOG A INNER JOIN CATALOG B
    ON A.SUB# = B.CATLG#
 WHERE A.SUB# <> ' '

SELECT A.CATLG#,A.CATDSC,A.SUB#,B.CATDSC
  FROM CATALOG A, CATALOG B
 WHERE A.SUB# <> ' '
   AND A.SUB# = B.CATLG#
```

This statement produces the results in Table 6.5.

TABLE 6.5
Results of the SELECT Statement in Example 7

CATLG#	CATDSC	SUB#	CATDSC
A597-3996A	Sahara Desert Mummy Sleeping Bag	B156-3780A	Arctic Circle Mummy Sleeping Bag
A483-7921B	Case 10W40 Motor Oil	B489-7920B	Case 10W30 Motor Oil

JOINING RESULTING TABLES

You may encounter situations where you are executing different SELECT statements and you need to combine the results. The UNION clause gives you this capability.

You might need to use the UNION clause when the question posed requires two or more distinct actions. The request is not really a join function; however, the results are to be combined. In a case like this, the UNION clause can help you extract these data requests.

The UNION Clause

The UNION clause lets you combine the results of two or more SELECT statements into one resulting table. The fields listed in each SELECT clause must match in order and type. For example, you cannot have a numeric value in the same relative column as a character value.

The syntax of the UNION clause is

```
UNION [ALL]
```

When you use the UNION clause, duplicate records in the final resulting table will be dropped, unless you specify the ALL keyword. When every field has the same value for two or more records, only one record is placed in the final table.

The UNION clause causes the table to be sorted. The sort will be based on the order of the fields in the resulting table unless you specify the ORDER BY clause. If you use the ALL keyword, the resulting table not will be sorted unless you specify the ORDER BY clause.

The maximum number of SELECT statements that can be joined is 32. Also, the total number of files that can be specified (joined or otherwise) for all the SELECT statements is 32.

1. If you need to produce a list of all the numbers of catalog items that were sold during 1991 or were introduced into the catalog master file after 1990, you can use the following statement:

```
SELECT DISTINCT CATLG#
  FROM SALESHST
 WHERE SHPDTE BETWEEN 910101 AND 911231
UNION
SELECT CATLG#
  FROM CATALOG
 WHERE SUBSTR(DIGITS(CATDTE),5,2) > '90'
```

The records this statement selects are listed in Table 6.6.

TABLE 6.6
Results of the SELECT Statement in Example 1

From SALESHST CATLG#	From CATALOG CATLG#
A225-8037A	A483-7921B
A483-7921B	B489-7920B
A597-3996A	B156-3780A
A658-4077A	D362-7997A
B115-3170A	
B156-3780A	
B489-7920B	
B501-1218D	
C689-1192D	
C871-1139C	
D805-0271C	

The statement produces the final results listed in Table 6.7.

TABLE 6.7

The Final Results of the SELECT Statement in Example 1

CATLG#
A225-8037A
A483-7921B
A597-3996A
A658-4077A
B115-3170A
B156-3780A
B489-7920B
B501-1218D
C689-1192D
C871-1139C
D362-7997A
D805-0271C

If you were to execute this same statement with the ALL keyword, Table 6.8 will be extracted.

TABLE 6.8

The Final Results of the SELECT Statement Using the All Keyword

CATLG#
A225-8037A
A483-7921B
A597-3996A
A658-4077A
B115-3170A
B156-3780A
B489-7920B
B501-1218D
C689-1192D
C871-1139C
C805-0271C
A483-7921B
B489-7920B
B156-3780A
D362-7997A

Notice in this last table that the results were not sorted and duplicate records are present.

2. Assume you want a list of the total dollars for orders by part, but you also want to see the total dollars for each part sold, even if there are no open orders. To produce this list, you could use the following statement:

```
SELECT CATLG#, 'Open Order $:',
       SUM((ORDQTY-SHPQTY)*PRICE)
          AS "Amount"
  FROM ORDERITM
 WHERE STATUS = 'O'
 GROUP BY CATLG#
UNION
SELECT CATLG#, 'Amount Sold:', CURYR$
  FROM CATALOG
 ORDER BY 1,2
```

This statement produces the results in Table 6.9.

TABLE 6.9
Results of the SELECT Statement in Example 2

CATLG#		Amount
A225-8037A	Amount Sold:	4030.00
A483-7921B	Amount Sold:	1039.35
A483-7921B	Open Order$:	1039.35
A597-3996A	Amount Sold:	0.00
A658-4077A	Amount Sold:	1964.25
B115-3170A	Amount Sold:	1056.00
B115-3170A	Open Order$:	220.00
B156-3780A	Amount Sold:	2999.70
B156-3780A	Open Order$:	2999.70
B489-7920B	Amount Sold:	1279.20
B501-1218D	Amount Sold:	3750.00
B501-1218D	Open Order$:	750.00
C689-1192D	Amount Sold:	2400.00
C871-1139C	Amount Sold:	1655.64
D362-7997A	Amount Sold:	270.00
D805-0271C	Amount Sold:	1550.53
D805-0271C	Open Order$:	1349.59

3. The following statement produces a detail list with intermediate totals. (NOTE: This method is an inefficient way to accomplish that goal. You are better off using Query Management, which allows for subtotaling.)

```
SELECT CTGRY#,' ',AMOUNT
  FROM SALESHST, CATALOG
 WHERE SHPDTE BETWEEN 910101 AND 910630
   AND SALESHST.CATLG# = CATALOG.CATLG#
UNION
SELECT CTGRY#,'Total for Category#:',SUM(AMOUNT)
  FROM SALESHST, CATALOG
 WHERE SHPDTE BETWEEN 910101 AND 910630
   AND SALESHST.CATLG# = CATALOG.CATLG#
 GROUP BY CTGRY#
```

This statement produces the results in Table 6.10.

TABLE 6.10

Results of the SELECT Statement in Example 3

CTGRY#		Amount
15		11523.60
15	Total for Category#:	11523.60
24		6500.00
24	Total for Category#:	6500.00
64		1470.00
64		4500.00
64	Total for Category#:	5970.00
156		3464.23
156	Total for Category#:	3464.23
348		3237.50
348	Total for Category#:	3237.50

Chapter 7

Subselects

The last topic we want to discuss related to data manipulation is subselects. Subselects, or *subqueries* as they are sometimes called, are SQL expressions that begin with the SELECT keyword and that define a result table. Subselects give you the capability to nest a SELECT statement within WHERE or HAVING clauses.

Before we go any further, we need to explain two terms: *outer select* and *inner select*. Outer select refers to the SELECT statement that is executing a nested SELECT statement. The nested SELECT statement is the inner select — in other words, the SELECT statement that is inside another SELECT.

Here's an example of coding a subselect:

```
SELECT CATLG#,CATDSC
  FROM CATALOG
  WHERE YR1$ < (SELECT AVG(YR1$)
                FROM CATALOG)
```

OVERVIEW

Subselects provide the capability to build a list of values dynamically and to perform a test against that list. When you nest a SELECT statement, you are instructing SQL that, for every record processed by the outer select, it is to execute an inner select and test the results.

When a subselect is executed, it can only return a single column in its resulting table. Any number of records can be included, but only a single column can be extracted unless you use the EXISTS predicate.

The entire SELECT statement allows a maximum of 32 subselects, including the UNION clause. The highest nesting level is 31, which means you can have up to 31 SELECT statements nested within each other. It is doubtful you would ever attempt this level of complexity, let alone reach this limit. Even under the most unusual circumstances, you probably won't exceed a nesting level of 4 or 5.

HOW SUBSELECTS ARE CODED

You code a subselect within the WHERE or HAVING clause and enclose it within parentheses. This lets SQL know where one SELECT statement begins and ends. The subselect always comes after a relational or special operator.

When you include the UPDATE or DELETE statement within a subselect, you cannot reference the updated file anywhere within the subselect, either directly or indirectly. One way to get around this limitation is to copy the file to another file name or library and then reference the newly created file in the subselect.

When you build the subselect, you can use only the following clauses:

SELECT Clause
FROM Clause
WHERE Clause
GROUP BY Clause
HAVING Clause

Basic Relational Testing

When you code a subselect using a relational operator, you must ensure that the result is a single record. This means that the subselect cannot extract more than one single value and that it can extract, at most, one record from the SELECT statement. Because you are testing a value with a condition such as equal to or greater than, you cannot have more than one record in the subselect table.

The syntax for the subselect is

```
expression {relational operator} (Sub-SELECT)
```

Typically, the subselect performs some kind of data summarization. You can use any type of data value with this operator. However, you must ensure that you are comparing like values. For example, if the expression is a numeric value, the subselect must provide a numeric value.

Quantified Relational Testing

A quantified relational test lets you perform a relational operator test over a list of values. When the relational test is performed, it is done for every record in the resulting table of the subselect.

The syntax for a quantified relational test operator is

```
expression {relational operator} [SOME | ANY | ALL]
        (Sub-SELECT)
```

By means of special operators, you now can have more than one record from the subselect to perform your relational test against. However, you still are limited to a single value being extracted.

You can use any type of data value with this operator, but you must ensure that you are comparing like values. For example, if the expression is a numeric value, the subselect must provide numeric values.

The ALL Operator

The ALL operator lets you use a relational operator against a subselect and determine whether the condition is true for all the values in the list. The operator will prove true if the relational test is true for all the values.

For example, if you use the "greater than" operator and the subselect builds a list with 10 values, the "greater than" test must be true for every value in the list. This would be equivalent to saying, "Value is greater than the first item in the list and value is greater than the second item in the list," and so on.

The SOME Operator

The SOME operator lets you use a relational operator against a subselect to determine whether the condition is true for some of the values. The operator will prove true if the relational test is true for at least one value in the list.

For example, if you use the "greater than" operator and the subselect builds a list with 10 values, the "greater than" test must be true for only one value in the list. This is equivalent to saying, "Value is greater than the first item in the list, or value is greater than the second item in the list," and so on.

The ANY Operator

The ANY operator is the same as the SOME operator.

SPECIAL SUBSELECT OPERATORS

Let's look at two other operators you can use for testing purposes: the EXISTS operator and the IN operator.

The EXISTS Operator

The EXISTS operator tests to see whether any records exist in a subselect. If any records were selected by the subselect, the condition is true. If you use the NOT keyword, the test is true only if no records were selected by the subselect.

The syntax of the EXISTS operator is

```
[NOT] EXISTS (Sub-SELECT)
```

This operator is the only one that does not require you to select a single value for the resulting table. Because you are only testing the existence of records, you can use the * or any other fields you may want. Because the fields in the subselect have no meaning to the EXISTS operator, you can specify anything you want.

Every record processed by the outer select will either pass or fail the EXISTS test depending on whether data is selected by the subselect.

The IN Operator

Recall from Chapter 3 that the IN operator checks to see whether a value is in a specified list. With subselect, you now have the capability to build a dynamic list of values instead of hardcoding the list.

The syntax of the IN operator is

```
expression [NOT] IN (Sub-SELECT)
```

The subselect checks the expression against the list built by the subselect. If any entry in the subselect equals the value of the expression, the result is true. You have the capability to negate this test by using the NOT keyword. When you use the NOT keyword, the test will be true if none of the entries in the list are equal to the expression.

You can use any type of data value with the IN operator; however, you must ensure that you are comparing like values. For example, if the expression is a numeric value, the subselect must provide a numeric value.

METHODS FOR EXECUTING A SUBSELECT

There are several methods for executing a subselect; we discuss each here and provide examples of how they look and act when executed.

Single-Value Testing

You can use a subselect to produce a single value and then perform a test against it. In this case, you can use any of the relational operators against the result.

1. Let's say you want to list every item in the catalog master file where last year's sales were less than the average sales for the same year. To do this, you could enter the following statement:

```
SELECT CATLG#,CATDSC
  FROM CATALOG
 WHERE YR1$ < (SELECT AVG(YR1$) FROM CATALOG)
```

This statement produces the results in Table 7.1.

TABLE 7.1
Results of the SELECT Statement in Example 1

CATLG#	CAATDSC
A597-3996A	Sahara Desert Mummy Sleeping Bag
B115-3170A	Baroque Bead Necklace
D805-0271C	Vinyl Bean Bag Chair
C871-1139C	Corduroy Bean Bag Chair
A483-7921B	Case 10W40 Motor Oil
B489-7920B	Case 10W30 Motor Oil
B156-3780A	Arctic Circle Mummy Sleeping Bag
D362-7997A	Portable CD Player

2. Now let's say you want to list the average sales last year for every category in the catalog master file where that average is less than the average sales for the last three years. The following statement will accomplish this objective:

```
SELECT CTGRY#,AVG(YR1$)
  FROM CATALOG
 GROUP BY CTGRY#
HAVING AVG(YR1$) < (SELECT AVG(CURYR$+YR1$+YR2$) FROM CATALOG)
```

This statement produces the results in Table 7.2.

TABLE 7.2
Results of the SELECT Statement in Example 2

CTGRY#	AVG(YR1R$)
15	5351.09333333
38	1869.00000000
64	6889.00000000
156	2616.82000000
348	2913.75000000

Simple List of Values

You can use a subselect to produce a list of values and then check to see whether a condition is true against the list. In this case you must use one of the quantified or special operators available.

1. Let's say you need to know when a record in the order header file does not have a corresponding record in the order item file. You can use the following statement to accomplish this task:

```
SELECT ORDER#,CUST#
  FROM ORDERHDR
  WHERE ORDER# NOT IN (SELECT ORDER# FROM ORDERITM)
```

The inner select builds a list of every order number in the order item file. Then each record in the order header file is checked to see whether the order number is in the list built.

2. If you want to know which customers in the customer master file have open orders in the order header file, you can enter the following statement:

```
SELECT CUST#,NAME
  FROM CUSTMAST
  WHERE CUST# IN (SELECT CUST# FROM ORDERHDR WHERE STATUS = 'O')
```

The subselect builds a table of all the customer numbers in the order header file where the status of the order is open (O) (see Table 7.3 on page 102). Then each customer record is tested to see whether it matches one of the numbers in the subselect. If it matches, the customer record is selected.

TABLE 7.3

Results of the SELECT Statement in Example 2

CUST#	NAME
392	Jane's Gift Emporium
411	Bob & Carol's Hallway Gifts
1583	Paul's Auto Store
8395	Alice's Sundries
32418	Hemingway Travel Club
62990	Bar & Grill Health Club

Data-Correlation Testing

Data-correlation testing lets you use data from an outer select to help you determine whether records are selected within the subselect. This method lets you perform a type of joining operation without having to specify the join in the outer SELECT.

To use data from an outer select, you must use a correlated name in the FROM clause of the SELECT statement. SQL uses this alias to qualify where the data is coming from.

You can use data testing whether you are extracting a single value or a list of values within the subselect. In other words, you can perform data correlation testing regardless of the type of subselect you are using.

In the following examples, pay close attention to how the data is used to perform the subselect.

1. The following statement selects every order in the order header file where a record does not exist in the order item file for that order.

```
SELECT ORDER#,CUST#
  FROM ORDERHDR A
  WHERE ORDER# NOT IN (SELECT ORDER# FROM ORDERITM
                        WHERE ORDER# = A.ORDER#)
```

Every time a record is read from the outer select, the inner select is executed. The inner select builds a list of order numbers where the order number is equal to the order number from the outer select. By using NOT IN for our test, the test will prove true and the record will be selected by the outer select if no records are extracted by the inner select. The statement in this example produces the following table:

ORDER#	CUST#
1411	411

2. The following statement performs the same test as the previous example, except we are using a different operator to perform the test:

```
SELECT ORDER#,CUST#
  FROM ORDERHDR A
 WHERE NOT EXISTS (SELECT ORDER# FROM ORDERITM
                    WHERE ORDER# = A.ORDER#)
```

As expected, the results are the same as for the previous statement:

ORDER#	CUST#
1411	411

3. If you want to delete any records in the order header where there were no corresponding records in the order item file, you can enter this statement:

```
DELETE FROM ORDERHDR A
 WHERE ORDER# NOT IN (SELECT ORDER# FROM ORDERITM
                       WHERE ORDER# = A.ORDER#)
```

In our sample database, one record is deleted.

4. If you want to know which items in the catalog master file have enough quantity on hand to cover at least one open order in the order item file for that item, you can use the following statement:

```
SELECT CATLG#,ONHAND
  FROM CATALOG A
 WHERE ONHAND > SOME (SELECT ORDQTY-SHPQTY FROM ORDERITM
                       WHERE STATUS = 'O' AND CATLG# = A.CATLG#)
```

This statement produces the results in Table 7.4.

TABLE 7.4
Results of the SELECT Statement in Example 4

CATLG#	ONHAND
B115-3170A	147
B501-1218D	150
D805-0271C	14
B156-3780A	50

5. Now let's say you want to know which items in the catalog master file do not have enough on hand stock to ship even one open order in the order item file. You can use this statement to find the answer:

```
SELECT CATLG#,ONHAND
  FROM CATALOG A
 WHERE ONHAND < ALL (SELECT ORDQTY-SHPQTY FROM ORDERITM
                      WHERE STATUS = 'O' AND CATLG# = A.CATLG#)
```

This statement produces the results in Table 7.5.

TABLE 7.5
Results of the SELECT Statement in Example 5

CATLG#	ONHAND
A597-3996A	0
A225-8037A	1500
C689-1192D	189
C871-1139C	15
A658-4077A	100
A483-7921B	35
B489-7920B	30
D362-7997A	250

6. If you want to know which customers in the customer master file have at least one open order in the order header file, you can enter the following statement:

```
SELECT CUST#,NAME
  FROM CUSTMAST A
 WHERE EXISTS (SELECT * FROM ORDERHDR WHERE STATUS = 'O'
               AND CUST# = A.CUST#)
```

This statement produces the results in Table 7.6.

TABLE 7.6
Results of the SELECT Statement in Example 6

CUST#	NAME
392	Jane's Gift Emporium
411	Bob & Carol's Hallway Gifts
1583	Paul's Auto Store
8395	Alice's Sundries
32418	Hemingway Travel Club
62990	Bar & Grill Health Club

Chapter 8

Data Definition Language

In addition to manipulating an existing database with SQL, you can use SQL to create a new database. In this chapter, we introduce the concepts and the statements related to creating an SQL database. We also discuss stored procedures, because you normally use stored procedures when you define the rules and processes associated with a database.

Five distinct types of objects are involved with SQL databases: collections, aliases, tables, indexes, and views. We discuss each type in the following sections.

COLLECTIONS

A collection is a repository where SQL-created objects are stored. A collection is the same as a library, and, in fact, when you create a collection, the object type created is *LIB. Because a collection is a library, you can perform any functions on an SQL collection that you can perform on any AS/400 library.

When you create an SQL collection, however, many additional objects are created. SQL uses these additional objects to track all the tables, indexes, and views within the SQL collection, as well as other special attributes of the database.

When you create a collection, SQL creates special database files called *catalogs*. These catalogs log information about every file, logical, and view created within the collection. Table 8.1 describes the catalogs SQL creates within the collection.

TABLE 8.1
The Various Catalogs Created by SQL in a Collection

Catalog name	Catalog contents
SYSCHKCST	Descriptions of every check constraint defined in every database file in the collection
SYSCOLUMNS	Descriptions of every column in every database file in the collection
SYSCST	Descriptions of every constraint put on a table in the collection
SYSCSTCOL	Descriptions of every constraint put on a column in the collection
SYSCSTDEP	Descriptions of every constraint dependency put on a table in the collection
SYSINDEXES	Descriptions of every index in the collection
SYSKEYCST	Descriptions of every constraint put on a key in the collection
SYSKEYS	Descriptions of every key used in the collection
SYSPACKAGES	Descriptions of every package in the collection
SYSREFCST	Descriptions of every referential constraint put on a table in the collection
SYSTABLES	Descriptions of every table in the collection
SYSVIEWDEP	Descriptions of the dependencies of every view in the collection
SYSVIEWS	Descriptions of every view in the collection

In addition to the catalog files created within the collection, there are system-level catalog files that reside in QSYS2. These system-level catalog files contain information about every file within the system — not just about a single collection. QSYS2 also contains three additional catalogs, listed in Table 8.2.

TABLE 8.2
Three Additional Catalogs Contained in QSY2

Catalog name	Catalog contents
SQL_LANGUAGES	Descriptions of the languages available on the AS/400
SYSPARMS	Descriptions of parameters used by stored procedures on the AS/400
SYSPROCS	Descriptions of every stored procedure on the AS/400

Any time you create, rename, or move a file, or perform any operation against a file in an SQL collection, the operating system automatically updates the catalog entries for that collection. Because of these updates, such operations can take much longer than they otherwise would. For example, whether or not SQL created a database file, if you move that file into or out of an SQL collection, the appropriate catalog files will be updated.

In addition to the catalog files created, an SQL collection contains a journal and a journal receiver. Every file SQL creates into that collection will be automatically journaled. The name of the journal file is QSQJRN and the journal receiver is QSQJRN0001.

Because every SQL-created file is automatically journaled, you also can automatically perform commitment control against those files. (See Chapter 9 for more information about commitment control.)

SQL provides no additional processing for controlling the journal or the journal receiver.

ALIASES

An alias is a special DDM file created as a reference name to a table or view. With aliases, you can specify which member is to be processed for a multiple member file.

Aliases can only reference tables or views on the current server. If you reference a distributive data file, only the file on the current server is referenced by the alias.

SQL treats the alias name the same as any other table name. Anywhere you can reference a table or a view, you can use an alias name.

Aliases are created with the CREATE ALIAS command.

TABLES

An SQL table is a physical file where data is stored. When you create a table, the object type is a physical file (*PF). Because of this, any operation you can perform on a physical file you can also perform on an SQL table.

SQL lets you dynamically add or drop columns (fields) in a table, changing the row (record) layout without having to re-create the table.

SQL also lets you place referential integrity on a table or column. Referential integrity encompasses the rules by which one table is dependent on another table. You achieve referential integrity by placing valid constraints on the tables within a collection. These constraints define what is to happen when a row is added, deleted, or updated. Once you have defined the constraints, the system uses them to ensure the integrity of the tables, even if SQL statements do not perform the updates. And because the referential integrity rules are contained in system-level catalogs, you are not limited to specifying these constraints only on SQL-created tables, but on other files as well.

When you have defined the constraints properly, the relationships between tables will be properly maintained when data is added to, updated, or deleted from the database. You also can ensure that if a column contains a value that must exist in another table, you can enforce this rule. For example, let's say you have a column defined as a part number. You can ensure that this column cannot be updated unless there is a corresponding row in another table — for example, the part master table.

It's important that you don't confuse referential integrity with triggers. Referential integrity specifies rules to be followed any time a row is added, updated, or deleted. If an action violates a referential constraint, the action is not taken. Triggers, on the other hand, are programs that are automatically called either before or after a row is added, updated, or deleted. Referential constraints are defined by the CREATE TABLE and ALTER TABLE statements explained later in this chapter.

At times, the integrity of a table might become questionable as a result of actions such as a disk failure or restoring a table that may or may not meet the referential constraints defined. In cases such as these, the system will place the table in a "check pending" status, which means that no input or output operations — and only read and insert operations — are allowed against the parent table.

To correct a table in this state, you must disable the constraint relationship between the two tables using the CHGPFCST (Change Physical File Constraint) command, correct the keys in question, then enable the constraint again. You can determine which rows are in violation by using the DSPCPCST (Display Check Pending Constraint) command.

INDEXES

Indexes are SQL objects that let you specify a special sorting sequence on a table. An index is exactly the same as a logical file. When an index is built, the object type is a logical file; any operations that are valid for a logical file are also valid for an index.

You can create an index over any valid AS/400 physical file, even a file not created with SQL. When you create an index, it is not journaled automatically. If you want to journal an index, you must specify this by hand. You cannot place referential constraints on an index.

VIEWS

A view is a special SQL object that lets you create a SELECT statement and attach that statement to a logical file. The best way to think of a view is as a select/omit (join) logical file.

When you create a view, the object type is a logical file. However, if you examine the attributes of the file, you will notice a special entry that describes the SQL SELECT statement attached to this view. Because a view is really a cross between a physical file and a logical file, you will find that some information normally associated with a logical file will be missing in a view. For example, you will not find any fields listed for the keyed index. And because the view is a logical file, an index and a view cannot have the same name within the same collection.

One interesting aspect of a view is that every time either SQL or an HLL program opens the view, a query select is executed. This is necessary because the system does not maintain a permanent index for a view.

Some views may be read-only, which means you cannot perform any INSERT, UPDATE, or DELETE statements against the view. Also, HLL update or delete operations are allowed. A view is read-only if any of the following conditions are true in the SELECT statement:

- You are joining files together
- The file specified in the SELECT is a read-only view
- You use the DISTINCT keyword
- You perform data summarization
- You use the same database file within an outer select and an inner select

STORED PROCEDURES

A stored procedure is any type of program on the AS/400 that you define to an SQL database and that you can call with an SQL statement. The system-level catalog files hold information about stored procedures.

Use the CREATE PROCEDURE statement to define stored procedures; use the CALL statement to execute them.

SQL STATEMENTS

Following are the SQL statements you can use when defining an SQL database. They are listed alphabetically.

The ALTER TABLE Statement

The ALTER TABLE statement is a powerful tool for maintaining an existing database file. You can use this statement to add or drop fields to or from a file, add or drop referential constraints, or even change the attributes of a field.

1. This statement adds a field called SALES# to the CATALOG file. The field is defined as a small integer.

```
ALTER TABLE CATALOG
       ADD COLUMN SALES# INT
```

2. This statement deletes the field SALES# from the CATALOG file.

```
ALTER TABLE CATALOG
       DROP COLUMN SALES#
```

Figure 8.1 is a comprehensive example of the ALTER TABLE statement.

FIGURE 8.1
An Example of the ALTER TABLE Statement

```
ALTER TABLE file name    [ADD COLUMN                      |
                          ALTER COLUMN                    |
                          DROP COLUMN                     |
                          ADD unique constraint           |
                          ADD referential constraint      |
                          DROP constraint] ... ]

ADD [COLUMN] column name [FOR [COLUMN] system-column-name]
        data type [NOT NULL] |
                   [[WITH] DEFAULT [value |
                                    NULL |
                                    CURRENT_DATE |
                                    CURRENT_TIME |
                                    CURRENT_TIMESTAMP]]    |
                   [CONSTRAINT constraint name] |
                   [UNIQUE |
                   [PRIMARY KEY |
                   [REFERENCES file name [(column name [, ...])]
                              [ON DELETE [RESTRICT |
                                          CASCADE  |
                                          NO ACTION |
                                          SET NULL |
                                          SET DEFAULT]]
                              [ON UPDATE [NO ACTION |
                                          RESTRICT]]]
[CHECK check condition]]]]]
```

continued

FIGURE 8.1 CONTINUED

```
ALTER [COLUMN] column name ([SET [DATA TYPE data type |
                            [WITH] DEFAULT [value |
                                           NULL |
                                           CURRENT_DATE |
                                           CURRENT_TIME |
                                           CURRENT_TIMESTAMP]] |

                      NOT NULL] |
                    [DROP [DEFAULT | NOT NULL]] ...)

DROP [COLUMN] column name [CASCADE | RESTRICT]

ADD [CONSTRAINT constraint name]
    {UNIQUE | PRIMARY KEY} (column name [, ...])]

ADD [CONSTRAINT constraint name] [FOREIGN KEY]
    (column [, ...]) [REFERENCES file name [(column name [, ...])]
                                    [ON DELETE [RESTRICT |
                                                CASCADE |
                                                SET NULL |
                                                SET DEFAULT |
                                                NO ACTION]] |
                                    [ON UPDATE [RESTRICT |
                                                NO ACTION]]]

DROP PRIMARY KEY

DROP [FOREIGN KEY | UNIQUE | CHECK | CONSTRAINT] constraint name
                  [CASCADE | RESTRICT]
```

The ALTER TABLE statement has seven basic components, which we discuss below. Within a single ALTER TABLE statement you can specify as many of these components as you wish, and in any order. If you are making several changes to a file, you probably will want to issue a single ALTER TABLE statement and several statements at once. This is especially true when you are adding or dropping fields from the file.

Let's look at each individual construct of the ALTER TABLE statement.

ADD COLUMN

You use this construct to add a field to a file. You specify the name of the field to add. You can specify an AS/400 field name (i.e., 10-character name) to the field using the FOR COLUMN subclause. If you don't specify a valid system field name, SQL will generate a field.

You must then specify the data type for the field. For a list of the valid data types, see the CREATE TABLE statement later in this chapter.

The NOT NULL subclause prevents the field from containing null values. The default is to allow null values. If you specify NOT NULL, you must specify the DEFAULT subclause.

The DEFAULT subclause specifies what value the field will contain when a record is added to the file with no specified value. You can specify a constant value, a NULL value, or the current date, time, or timestamp value (CURRENT_DATE, CURRENT_TIME, CURRENT_TIMESTAMP).

When you add a field, you can use the CONSTRAINT subclause to apply a referential constraint to this field.

In addition, you can specify whether this field is a UNIQUE key for the file or the PRIMARY KEY for the file. You cannot specify UNIQUE and PRIMARY KEY for the same field, nor can you specify either UNIQUE or PRIMARY KEY for more than one field.

If you don't specify a UNIQUE or PRIMARY KEY, you can define a foreign key for this field using the REFERENCES subclause. This subclause defines the fields that are foreign keys to this field and what actions, if any, are to be taken when a record is updated or deleted in this file.

ALTER COLUMN

ALTER COLUMN lets you change the attributes of an already existing field. You can change the data type of the field with the SET DATA TYPE subclause. For a list of the valid data types, see the CREATE TABLE statement later in this chapter. Note that the data type you change the field to must be compatible with the current data type defined for the field.

You can set this field's default value with the DEFAULT subclause. The SET NOT NULL subclause specifies that the field cannot contain null values. The DROP DEFAULT subclause drops the current default setting for the field. DROP NOT NULL will change the field to allow null values.

DROP COLUMN

This construct deletes a field from the file. If the field in question has any referential constraints defined, you must define the action to be taken with any dependent objects. CASCADE specifies that all dependent objects will be deleted. RESTRICT specifies that the field will not be deleted unless all dependencies on the field are removed.

ADD Unique Constraint

This construct defines the keys used for this file. The keys are contained within a constraint name. You can either specify the name of the constraint using the CONSTRAINT subclause or you can let the system generate a name.

Next you must specify a group of fields that will make up the key of this file. You must specify whether the fields are a UNIQUE key group or a PRIMARY KEY group. You cannot specify UNIQUE and PRIMARY KEY for the same field.

ADD Referential Constraint

This construct defines a referential constraint for the file. You can specify the name of the constraint with the CONSTRAINT subclause, or you can let the system generate a name.

The FOREIGN KEY subclause specifies the field names that make up this referential constraint. You specify each column name, separated by commas. Then you use the REFERENCES subclause to define the file name that is dependent on these sets of fields. You also can define what actions are to be taken on the dependent file when a record in this file is updated or deleted.

DROP KEY

This construct deletes the primary key for the file. You specify the PRIMARY KEY subclause. When you use the DROP key, all referential constraints defined on the primary key also will be deleted.

DROP CONSTRAINT

This construct deletes any referential constraints defined on the file. You can specify either FOREIGN KEY, UNIQUE, or a specific constraint name.

FOREIGN KEY specifies the name of a constraint on which this table is dependent. UNIQUE drops the unique key, but will not drop the primary key for the file. CONSTRAINT specifies the name of a constraint to delete.

The CALL Statement

The CALL statement calls a stored procedure. You can optionally pass parameters to the stored procedure. You define the procedure to SQL via the CREATE PROCEDURE statement. However, you can call any valid AS/400 program, even if the program is not defined to SQL. In addition to using the CALL statement in an interactive SQL session, you can call a stored procedure from within an HLL program (we discuss this process in Chapter 11).

The syntax of the CALL statement is

```
CALL procedure  [(parameter [,...])]
```

An example of a CALL statement is

```
CALL PROGRAMA
```

The COMMENT ON Statement

Use the COMMENT ON statement to enter comments within a file. SQL places these comments in the catalog files within the collection where the file resides. You can view the comments only from the catalog files; they do not appear at any other time when you are working on the file.

The following examples show how you can enter comments against the catalog master file:

1. ```
   COMMENT ON TABLE CATALOG IS 'Catalog Master File'
   ```

2. ```
   COMMENT ON CATALOG
             (CATLG# IS 'Catalog Number',
              CATDSC IS 'Description',
              CATDTE IS 'Date entered catalog (MDY)',
   ```

```
CTGRY# IS 'Category Number',
CURYR$ IS 'Sales for Current Year',
YR1$ IS 'Sales for 1 year ago',
YR2$ IS 'Sales for 2 years ago',
ONHAND IS 'Quantity on hand',
CPRICE IS 'Current Price',
FPRICE IS 'Future Price',
PRCDTE IS 'Date future price effective (YMD),
SUB# IS 'Substitute catalog number')
```

Syntax samples for the COMMENT ON statement include the following:

```
COMMENT ON {TABLE file name |
            ALIAS alias-name |
            INDEX file name |
            COLUMN file name.field name |
            PACKAGE package name |
            PROCEDURE procedure name |
            PARAMETER procedure name.parameter name} IS string
```

or

```
    COMMENT ON  [COLUMN] file name (field name IS string [,...])
```

or

```
    COMMENT ON  procedure name (parameter name IS string [,...])
```

The TABLE clause is valid only for an SQL table or view, or for an AS/400 physical file. Use the COLUMN clause to define a comment against a single field within a single file. In this case, you specify the name of the file, a period, then the name of the field (e.g., FILE.FIELD). There are no embedded blanks in this form. The ALIAS clause specifies a comment against an SQL-created alias. The PACKAGE clause specifies a comment against an SQL-created package (we discuss packages in Chapter 10). The PROCEDURE clause defines a comment against a defined SQL procedure. Use the PARAMETER clause to enter a comment against a single parameter defined within a procedure.

The second form of the COLUMN clause enters comments against as many fields as you wish. The second form of the PARAMETER clause enters comments against as many parameters as you wish. The comment you add cannot exceed a length of 2,000 characters. The file to which you are adding comments must reside within an SQL collection. Otherwise, the statement will execute but no catalog updates will be performed — and you are given no indication when this happens.

The CREATE ALIAS Statement

The CREATE ALIAS statement creates a special DDM file which is used to reference a table or view within a collection. The syntax of the CREATE ALIAS statement is

```
    CREATE ALIAS alias name  FOR [file name[(member name)] | view]
```

After the FOR clause, you will specify either a table name or a view name that is referenced by this alias. For a table, you can specify an optional member name, within parentheses.

The following is an example of the CREATE ALIAS statement:

```
CREATE ALIAS  MEMBER1 FOR FILEA(MEMBER1)
```

The CREATE COLLECTION Statement

The CREATE COLLECTION statement creates an SQL collection or library. The library name you specify must meet AS/400 naming standards. The syntax of the CREATE COLLECTION statement is

```
CREATE COLLECTION library name [IN ASP integer]
           [WITH DATA DICTIONARY]
```

Using the IN ASP keyword, you can direct the creation to a specific auxiliary storage pool defined on your AS/400.

The WITH DATA DICTIONARY option specifies that an IDDU data dictionary is to be created with this library in addition to the catalog files already created.

```
1. CREATE COLLECTION PRODLIB
```

The CREATE INDEX Statement

The CREATE INDEX statement creates a logical file over a physical file (any valid physical file, whether or not SQL created it). The syntax of the CREATE INDEX statement is

```
CREATE [UNIQUE [WHERE NOT NULL] | ENCODED VECTOR]
    INDEX index name   ON file name (field name [ASC | DESC],...)
```

1. If you want to have an index over a catalog master file sorted by category number and then by catalog number, you can issue this statement:

```
CREATE UNIQUE INDEX CATINDX1 ON CATALOG
            (CTGRY#,CATLG#)
```

2. If you also need a logical file over the catalog master file sorted by descending current-year sales and then by catalog number, you can issue this statement:

```
CREATE INDEX CATINDX2 ON CATALOG
            (CURYR$ DESC, CATLOG#)
```

If you want a logical file with a unique index, you use the UNIQUE keyword. Use the UNIQUE keyword to indicate that duplicate index values in the physical file are not allowed.

If a file contains fields that are null-capable and you want to build an index over one of those fields, you must remember that a null value is considered a specific value. If you specify UNIQUE and two or more rows contain null values, the index will not be built. You can use the WHERE NOT NULL keywords to specify that null values are not to be considered when uniqueness of the database records is determined.

You can specify that the index created is to use the encoded vector index scheme available on the AS/400 starting with V4R3 of the operating system. An encoded vector index is a special index used to improve performance. It does not provide a specific order to the records in the file. You cannot specify more than one file on the CREATE INDEX statement, which does not let you join files together.

The fields you specify for the index must follow the same rules as those you follow when you build an AS/400 logical file. You cannot have more than 120 fields specified, and the total length of all fields in the index cannot exceed 2,000 characters. You also must specify at least one field name.

The default for the sorting sequence for the index is ascending. You can use the ASC and DESC keywords, respectively, to specify ascending or descending order.

The CREATE PROCEDURE Statement

The CREATE PROCEDURE statement defines a stored procedure to the SQL database. A stored procedure is simply an AS/400 program. The CALL statement executes the stored procedure.

1. `CREATE PROCEDURE PROGRAMA`

2. `CREATE PROCEDURE PROGRAMA RESULT SETS 2`

The syntax of the CREATE PROCEDURE statement is

```
CREATE PROCEDURE procedure name
            [([IN | OUT | INOUT] parameter data_type [,...])]
[RESULT {SET | SETS} integer]
[SPECIFIC  specific name]
[[NOT] DETERMINISTIC]
[CONTAINS SQL | NO SQL | READS SQL DATA | MODIFIES SQL DATA]
[[EXTERNAL | EXTERNAL NAME] program]
[LANGUAGE [C | C++ | CL | COBOL | COBOLLE | FORTRAN |
         PLI | REXX | RPG | RPGLE]]
[PARAMETER STYLE] [GENERAL | GENERAL WITH NULLS]
[VARIANT | NOT VARIANT]
```

Only the name of the procedure is required. If you don't specify any other parameters, by default the program name will be the same as the procedure name.

You can define the procedure's parameters immediately after the procedure name. You can specify a maximum of 255 parameters for a single procedure. Specify each parameter as an input (IN), output (OUT), or input-output (INOUT) parameter. The default is IN. You give each parameter a name and a data type when you define this procedure. For a list of the valid data types, see the CREATE TABLE statement in this chapter.

The RESULT SETS clause defines the number of result sets that will be returned from the procedure to a Client Access client. Result sets are only returned when the procedure is called from an AS/400 Client Access client.

The SPECIFIC clause defines a name that uniquely identifies the procedure.

The DETERMINISTIC clause indicates whether the procedure will return the same results when identical input parameters are provided to the procedure on successive calls. DETERMINISTIC indicates that the same results will be provided. NOT DETERMINISTIC indicates that the same results may not result.

The CONTAINS SQL clause indicates that the procedure does include embedded SQL statements.

The NO SQL clause indicates that the procedure does not contain any embedded SQL statements.

The READS SQL DATA clause indicates that data is read in the procedure via SQL statements.

The MODIFIES SQL DATA clause indicates that data is modified in the procedure via SQL statements.

If the name of the program is not the same as the procedure, you must specify the EXTERNAL NAME (or EXTERNAL) clause to link the actual AS/400 program name to the procedure name.

If you wish, you can specify the language used to create the AS/400 program. If you don't specify the language, the language will be derived from the AS/400 program object itself. If the program object does not specify the language type, SQL assumes the language is C.

The PARAMETER STYLE clause is optional and is used strictly in association with the GENERAL clause.

You use the GENERAL clause to specify that a simple call to the program is to be executed. No additional arguments are passed for indicator variables (we discuss indicator variables in Chapter 10).

GENERAL WITH NULLS specifies that an additional argument will be passed when indicator variables are used.

VARIANT or NOT VARIANT is an option that specifies whether the procedure will return the same result when it is called with identical input values. (VARIANT means that the results will not be the same. NOT VARIANT means that the results will always be the same.)

The CREATE SCHEMA Statement

The CREATE SCHEMA statement is a special SQL statement that lets you create a complete database with one statement. The CREATE SCHEMA statement is valid only with the RUNSQLSTM command. You enter this statement into a source member, and the RUNSQLSTM command executes it.

The syntax of the CREATE SCHEMA statement is

```
CREATE SCHEMA (library name | AUTHORIZATION user profile)
[IN ASP integer] [WITH DATA DICTIONARY]
```

```
[CREATE TABLE |
 CREATE ALIAS |
 CREATE INDEX |
 CREATE VIEW  |
 COMMENT ON   |
 LABEL ON     |
 GRANT ... ]
```

```
1. CREATE SCHEMA TESTLIB
   CREATE TABLE TESTFILE
                (FIELD1 CHAR (10) NOT NULL WITH DEFAULT,
                 FIELD2 DEC (3,0) NOT NULL WITH DEFAULT)
   CREATE INDEX TESTLGL ON TESTFILE
                (FIELD2 DESC)
   COMMENT ON TESTFILE IS 'Test File'
   GRANT ALL ON TESTFILE
```

With the CREATE SCHEMA statement, you create an SQL collection and any number of tables, indexes, or views. You can specify either the library name to be created or a user profile name with the AUTHORIZATION keyword.

If you specify AUTHORIZATION, the collection created will be the same as the user profile. The user profile owns all the objects created by CREATE SCHEMA. If you do not specify a user profile, the user executing the statement owns all objects.

Using the IN ASP keywords, you can specify in which auxiliary storage pool the collection will reside. If you specify the WITH DATA DICTIONARY keywords, an IDDU data dictionary is also created within the collection.

After the collection has been named, you can specify any of the following statements:

- CREATE TABLE
- CREATE ALIAS
- CREATE INDEX
- CREATE VIEW
- COMMENT ON
- LABEL ON
- GRANT

You can specify as many of these statements as you wish, but the total length of the CREATE SCHEMA statement cannot exceed 32,766 characters.

The rules for specifying the SQL statements within the CREATE SCHEMA are the same as using them individually, except those for the COMMENT ON and LABEL ON statements: You cannot specify a package name when you use those statements within the CREATE SCHEMA statement.

All objects the CREATE SCHEMA statement creates will default to the collection created. If you specify a library name within any statement, that name must be the same as the collection name in the CREATE SCHEMA statement.

The CREATE TABLE Statement

The CREATE TABLE statement creates a table or physical file. Following the file name, you must specify every field this physical file will contain. You also can specify any unique constraints or referential constraints to be applied to this file.

See Figure 8.2 for the syntax of the CREATE TABLE statement.

FIGURE 8.2
The Syntax of the CREATE TABLE Statement

```
CREATE TABLE <library/>file name
           ([column_name [FOR [COLUMN] system_field_name] data_type
                [NOT NULL |
                 [WITH] DEFAULT [value |
                                 NULL |
USER   |

                                 CURRENT_DATE   |
                                 CURRENT_TIME   |
                                 CURRENT_TIMESTAMP]  |
                [CONSTRAINT constraint name]  |
                [UNIQUE  |
                [PRIMARY KEY  |
                [REFERENCES file name [(column name [, ...])]
                        [ON DELETE [RESTRICT   |
                                    CASCADE    |
                                    NO ACTION  |
                                    SET NULL   |
                                    SET DEFAULT]]
                        [ON UPDATE [NO ACTION |
                                    RESTRICT]]
                [CHECK  check condition] ... ]   |
[CONSTRAINT constraint name]
    {UNIQUE | PRIMARY KEY} (column name [, ...])  |
[CONSTRAINT constraint name]  FOREIGN KEY
    (column [, ...])
         [REFERENCES file name [(column name [, ...])]
                     [ON DELETE [RESTRICT   |
                                 CASCADE    |
                                 SET NULL   |
                                 SET DEFAULT |
                                 NO ACTION]]  |
                     [ON UPDATE [RESTRICT   |
                                 NO ACTION]]] [, ...])
[IN node group
    [PARTITIONING KEY (column [, ...]) [USING HASHING]]]
```

The following is an example using the CREATE TABLE statement to create the catalog database defined in Appendix A:

```
CREATE TABLE CATALOG
              (CATLG# CHAR (20) NOT NULL WITH DEFAULT,
               CATDSC CHAR (40) NOT NULL WITH DEFAULT,
        CATDTE NUMERIC (6,0) NOT NULL WITH DEFAULT,
               CTGRY# DEC (3,0) NOT NULL WITH DEFAULT,
```

```
CURYR$ DEC (7,2) NOT NULL WITH DEFAULT,
YR2$ DEC (7,2) NOT NULL WITH DEFAULT,
ONHAND DEC (7,0) NOT NULL WITH DEFAULT,
CPRICE DEC (7,2) NOT NULL WITH DEFAULT,
FPRICE DEC (7,2) NOT NULL WITH DEFAULT,
PRCDTE NUMERIC (6,0) NOT NULL WITH DEFAULT,
SUB# CHAR (20) NOT NULL WITH DEFAULT,
PRIMARY KEY(CATLG#))
```

Field Definitions

When you define field names to the file, you also must specify the data type of each field and the field's size, just as you would with DDS. If the field name you choose does not meet AS/400 naming standards, you can specify a system field name for the field by using the FOR COLUMN subclause. If you don't specify a valid system name, one will be generated automatically for you.

The following list provides information about the valid data types:

INTEGER — defines a large integer value.

INT — the same as INTEGER.

SMALLINT — defines a small integer value.

FLOAT [(precision)] — defines a floating-point value. If the precision is not entered or contains a value between 25 and 53, the number will be a double-precision, floating-point number. If the precision is between 1 and 24, the number will be a single-precision, floating-point number.

REAL — defines a single-precision, floating-point number.

DOUBLE PRECISION — defines a double-precision, floating-point number.

DOUBLE — the same as DOUBLE PRECISION.

DECIMAL [(length [,decimals])] — defines a packed-decimal field. If you do not specify the length of the number, the default will be 5 with 0 decimals. If you specify the length but do not specify the decimals, the default will be 0 decimals. The length can be any value between 1 and 31. If you specify both the length and the decimals, the decimals cannot be greater than the length of the number.

DEC — the same as DECIMAL.

NUMERIC [(length [,decimals])] — defines a zoned-decimal field. If you do not specify the length of the number, the default will be 5 with 0 decimals. If you specify the length but do not specify the decimals, the default will be 0 decimals. The length can be any value between 1 and 31. If you specify both the length and the decimals, the decimals cannot be greater than the length of the number.

CHARACTER [(length)] [FOR BIT DATA |
FOR SBCS DATA |
FOR MIXED DATA ccsid] — defines a fixed-length character value. If you do not specify the length, the default will be 1. The length specified can be any value between 1 and 32,766.

The second argument of this definition indicates the type of data that can be stored in this character field. FOR BIT DATA specifies that the data is not associated with any coded character sets and that character conversions are never performed. FOR SBCS DATA refers to a field that is stored using single-byte character set (SBCS) data representations. FOR MIXED DATA is used for a field that can contain both SBCS and double-byte character set (DBCS) data. With this argument, you must specify a valid coded-character-set identifier (CCSID).

CHAR — the same as CHARACTER.

VARCHAR (length) [ALLOCATE (length)]
[FOR BIT DATA |
FOR SBCS DATA |
FOR MIXED DATA ccsid] — defines a variable-length character string. You must specify a length between 1 and 32,740.

The ALLOCATE keyword tells how much space should be reserved for the field within the database record. When a character value is stored and it is less than the allocated size, the data is stored in the fixed portion of the database record. If the string is longer than the allocated size, the data is stored in the variable location for the record and requires more I/O to retrieve the record. If you do not specify an allocated length, the default is 0.

The second argument of this definition indicates the type of data that can be stored in this character field.

FOR BIT DATA specifies that the data is not associated with any coded character sets and that character conversions are never performed.

FOR SBCS DATA refers to a field that is stored using SBCS data representations.

FOR MIXED DATA refers to a field that can contain both SBCS and DBCS data. With this argument, you must specify a valid CCSID.

CHARACTER VARYING — the same as VARCHAR.

CHAR VARYING — the same as VARCHAR.

LONG VARCHAR — defines the field as a variable-length character field whose length is determined by the amount of space available for the row. The maximum length for a single row is 32,766 characters. If there are any variable-length fields defined in the row, the maximum length is 32,740 characters.

GRAPHIC [(length)] — defines a field as a DBCS field. If you do not specify the length, the default is 1. The length specified can be any value between 1 and 16,383. If the field is null-capable, the maximum length is 16,382 characters.

VARGRAPHIC (length) [ALLOCATE (length)] — defines a field as a variable-length DBCS field. You must specify a length and the value must be between 1 and 16,370. If the field is null-capable, the maximum length is 16,369 characters.

The ALLOCATE keyword designates the space to be reserved for the field within the database record. When a graphic character is stored that is less than the allocated size, the data is stored within a fixed portion of the database record. If the string is longer than the allocated size, the data is stored in the variable location for the record (more I/O is required for retrieving this data). If you do not specify an allocated size, the default is 0.

GRAPHIC VARYING — the same as VARGRAPHIC.

LONG VARGRAPHIC — defines the field as a variable-length graphic field whose length is determined by the amount of space available for the row. The maximum length for a single row is 32,766 characters. If there are any variable-length fields defined in the row, the maximum length is 32,740 characters.

DATE — defines a date field in ISO format (yyyy-mm-dd).

TIME — defines a time field in ISO format (hh.mm.ss).

TIMESTAMP — defines a timestamp field.

When you define field names to a file, you can specify a field as being null-capable. If you do not specify NOT NULL, the field will be null-capable.

You can specify what the default value should be when a record is added to the database file. If you don't specify a default value, the value will be based on the field's data type. If the field is null-capable, the default will be a null value.

If you specify a default value, that value can be a constant value, NULL for null values, CURRENT_DATE for a date field, CURRENT_TIME for a time field or CURRENT_TIMESTAMP for a timestamp field. If you specify DEFAULT, NULL and NOT NULL are mutually exclusive. Table 8.3 indicates what the default value would be.

TABLE 8.3
Default Values

Data Type	Default Value
Numeric	0
CHAR	blanks
VARCHAR	empty string
DATE	current date
TIME	current time
TIMESTAMP	current timestamp

Finally, you can specify any constraints to be placed on this field using the CONSTRAINT subclause. The constraint name you specify must be unique in the database. Once you specify a constraint, you must indicate the type of constraint that will be placed on this field.

PRIMARY KEY indicates that this field is used as the primary key for this file. When you specify PRIMARY KEY at the field level, you are indicating that the primary key for this file is a single field. If you specify PRIMARY KEY, you must use the NOT NULL clause.

UNIQUE indicates that this field defines a unique key for the file. When you specify UNIQUE KEY at the field level, you are indicating that this file has a unique key defined over a single field. PRIMARY KEY and UNIQUE are mutually exclusive.

You can specify a foreign key constraint via the REFERENCES subclause. To indicate the dependency, specify the name of the file and the field within that file.

Finally, you define what actions are to take place when a record is either updated or deleted from this file.

When a record is deleted, you can specify one of the following actions:

- ON DELETE NO ACTION indicates that no action is to take place in the dependent file.

- ON DELETE RESTRICT indicates that this record cannot be deleted if any foreign dependencies exist on this field.

- ON DELETE CASCADE indicates that all foreign dependency records will be deleted.

- ON DELETE SET NULL indicates that all fields dependent on this record are to have the values set to null.

- ON DELETE SET DEFAULT indicates that all fields dependent on this record are to be set to their default values.

When you are defining the actions that take place for a field update, you can specify one of the following actions:

- ON UPDATE NO ACTION indicates that no action is to take place when the value of the updated field changes.

- ON UPDATE RESTRICT indicates that the field will not be updated if any other fields are dependent on the current value of the field.

Unique Constraints

You define either a UNIQUE or a PRIMARY key for a file by defining a unique constraint. You can specify a constraint name for the file via the CONSTRAINT subclause. The name you specify must be unique within the database.

First, you specify whether this is a PRIMARY KEY or UNIQUE constraint. Then you specify all the fields that make up the key. You must list each field name within parentheses and separate the names by commas. PRIMARY KEY and UNIQUE are mutually exclusive.

PRIMARY KEY indicates that this set of fields is used as the primary key for this file. If you specify PRIMARY KEY, all the fields must be defined with the NOT NULL clause.

UNIQUE indicates that this field defines a unique key for the file. When you specify UNIQUE at the field level, you are indicating that this file has a unique key defined over a single field.

Referential Constraints

You define a referential constraint to specify which files are dependent on the file you are creating. You can specify a constraint name for the file via the CONSTRAINT subclause. The name you specify must be unique within the database.

Next, you must specify FOREIGN KEY, which tells SQL you are defining a referential constraint. Then you specify all the fields that make up the foreign key. List each field name within parentheses and separate the names with commas.

Finally, you use the REFERENCES subclause to define which file is dependent on this file. You specify the name of the dependent file and the fields within that file. The order and data types must match between the two files.

Within the REFERENCES subclause, you define what actions are to take place when a record is either updated or deleted from this file. When a record is deleted, you can specify one of the following actions:

- ON DELETE NO ACTION indicates that no action is to take place in the dependent file.
- ON DELETE RESTRICT indicates that the record cannot be deleted if there are any foreign dependencies on this field.
- ON DELETE CASCADE indicates that all foreign dependency records will be deleted.
- ON DELETE SET NULL indicates that the values of all fields dependent on this record will be set to null.
- ON DELETE SET DEFAULT indicates that the values of all fields dependent on this record will be set to the default.

When you are defining the actions that take place for a field update, you can specify one of the following actions:

- ON UPDATE NO ACTION indicates that no action will occur when the value of the updated field changes.
- ON UPDATE RESTRICT indicates that the field will not be updated if any other fields are dependent on the current value of the field.

After you define all of the fields and constraints for the database file, you can specify that this table is to be used as a distributive table across multiple AS/400s within a specific node group. The DB2 Multisystem for OS/400 product must be installed on your system for this to work (for more information about distributive database processing, see Chapter 9).

Within the IN subclause, you specify the name of the node group into which this distributive file is to be placed. The name of the node group must already exist.

After the IN subclause, you can define the partitioning key for this table. You use a partitioning key to determine on which node within the node group a row will be placed. You define the fields to be used within the PARTITIONING KEY subclause. Then you list the field names within parentheses and separate the names with commas. If you don't specify a partitioning key, the first field of the primary key determines the node in which to place the record. The fields you list for the partitioning key must be a subset of the fields defined within the unique constraint for this file.

The USING HASHING keywords indicate that the partitioning key will be hashed to determine where the row is placed within the node group.

The CREATE VIEW Statement

The CREATE VIEW statement creates an SQL view. The object created when you create a view is a logical file. The syntax of the CREATE VIEW statement is

```
CREATE VIEW view name [(field name [FOR [COLUMN] system
column,...)]
            AS Sub-SELECT
            [WITH [CASCADE | LOCAL] CHECK OPTION]
```

1. This view builds a logical view over the catalog master file, selecting every field where the current-year sales is 0. Using this statement is the same as creating a select/omit logical view.

```
CREATE VIEW CATVIEW1 AS
      SELECT *
        FROM CATALOG
      WHERE CURYR$=0
```

2. This view builds a logical over the catalog master file with three fields. The last field, TOTAL, is the sum of the current year's and previous two years' sales fields.

```
CREATE VIEW CATVIEW2 (CATLG#,CATDSC,TOTAL) AS
      SELECT CATLG#,CATDSC,CURYR$+YR1$+YR2$
        FROM CATALOG
```

3. This view builds a join logical over the catalog and category master files. Every field from both files is selected.

```
CREATE VIEW CATVIEW3 AS
      SELECT *
        FROM CATALOG, CATEGORY
       WHERE CATALOG.CTGRY# = CATEGORY.CTGRY#
```

4. This view builds a join logical over the catalog and category master files, selecting only the catalog number, category number, and category description.

```
CREATE VIEW CATVIEW4 AS
      SELECT CATLG#,A.CTGRY#,CTDESC
        FROM CATALOG A, CATEGORY B
       WHERE A.CTGRY# = B.CTGRY#
```

When you create a view, you can either specify the field names to use or you can let the subselect specify the field names. You must specify the names if the subselect uses a duplicate field name or has a calculated value in its list. You must ensure that the number of field names matches the number of returned values on the subselect.

If you define the field names and they do not meet AS/400 naming conventions, a default system field name is assigned. However, you can override this action by using the FOR COLUMN subclause, which lets you define the AS/400 field name to be used for the view.

The subselect that you specify is validated to ensure that all syntax and rules have been met. The subselect can use any of the clauses available on the SELECT statement except the ORDER BY and UNION clauses — exactly the same as when you use a subselect within the WHERE clause (see Chapter 7).

Note that some views may be considered *read-only*, which means you cannot perform any update operations to the view. You cannot use the INSERT, UPDATE, and DELETE statements against a read-only view. Likewise, you cannot use HLL update or delete operations.

A view is considered read-only if any of the following conditions are true on the SELECT statement:

- You are joining files together.
- The file specified in the SELECT is a read-only view.
- You use the DISTINCT keyword.
- You perform data summarization.
- You use the same database file within an outer select and an inner select.

Finally, when you define a view, you can specify whether constraints apply whenever a record is added or updated via the view. You do this via the WITH CHECK OPTION subclause. You cannot use the WITH CHECK OPTION subclause when the view is read-only.

You also can specify the words CASCADE or LOCAL after the word WITH. CASCADE indicates that every row that is updated or inserted must conform to the definition of the view. This designation prevents a row from becoming unavailable to the view. The LOCAL option is similar to CASCADE, except that a row might still become unavailable with the LOCAL option.

The DROP Statement

The DROP statement deletes any of the following objects: collection, schema, index, SQL package, stored-procedure definition, table, or SQL view. The syntax of the DROP statement is

```
DROP   [COLLECTION library name [CASCADE | RESTRICT]] |
       [SCHEMA library name [CASCADE | RESTRICT]] |
       [ALIAS  alias name] |
       [INDEX file name] |
       [PACKAGE package name] |
       [(PROCEDURE | ROUTINE) procedure name] |
       [SPECIFIC (PROCEDURE | ROUTINE) specific name] |
       [TABLE file name [CASCADE | RESTRICT]] |
       [VIEW file name {CASCADE | RESTRICT]]
```

1. This statement deletes the PRODLIB collection (library).

```
DROP COLLECTION PRODLIB
```

2. This statement deletes the catalog master file and any logical files, views, or indexes built over that file.

```
DROP TABLE CATALOG
```

3. This statement deletes the CATINDX2 logical file.

```
DROP INDEX CATINDX2
```

4. This statement deletes the CATVIEW1 view.

```
DROP VIEW CATVIEW1
```

The CASCADE/RESTRICT keywords, when allowed, define what happens to an object when referential constraints exist. CASCADE specifies that any tables, views, indexes, or referential constraints are also deleted when they are dependent on the object being deleted. RESTRICT specifies that the object cannot be deleted if any objects are dependent on it. In the case of a collection, this includes all dependencies on the tables and views within that collection.

The DROP COLLECTION statement is the same as the delete library (DLTLIB) command.

The DROP SCHEMA statement is the same as DROP COLLECTION.

The DROP ALIAS statement deletes an SQL alias.

The DROP INDEX statement is valid for any AS/400 logical file, even if SQL did not create the file.

The DROP PACKAGE statement deletes an SQL package (we discuss SQL packages in Chapter 10).

The DROP PROCEDURE statement deletes a stored-procedure definition from the database. The actual AS/400 program object is not deleted.

The DROP SPECIFIC statement deletes a specific procedure definition from the database.

The DROP TABLE statement not only deletes the file but also any indexes, views, and logical files that are built over the file. You can delete any AS/400 physical file, even if SQL did not create it.

The DROP VIEW statement is valid only for SQL-created views.

The GRANT Statement

The GRANT statement lets you assign AS/400 security rights to an SQL table, view, or physical file. Using this statement is similar to using the GRTOBJAUT (Grant Object Authority) command. The syntax of the GRANT statement is

```
GRANT {ALL [PRIVILEGES] |
           {{ALTER | DELETE | INDEX | INSERT |
            REFERENCES | SELECT | UPDATE},...}}
           ON [TABLE] {file name,...}
           TO {PUBLIC | user profile,...}
           [WITH GRANT OPTIONS]
```

By naming the files in the ON clause of this statement, you can specify any number of files to receive the authority.

1. This statement grants ALL rights to the catalog master file to the user profile USER1.

   ```
   GRANT ALL ON CATALOG TO USER1
   ```

You specify who is to receive the authority in the TO clause. You can grant the authority to PUBLIC or to any number of user profiles on the system. You cannot specify both PUBLIC and a user profile at the same time. If you specify ALL, you cannot specify any other rights, because they are mutually exclusive.

If you specify specific rights, you can list the authorities that are to be assigned. The authority required to assign rights to other users on the system is the same as it is anywhere else on the AS/400. You cannot assign to others any rights that you do not have.

The WITH GRANT OPTION indicates that the user profile who owns this object also can assign authority to other individuals.

Table 8.4 (on the following page) shows the relationship between the GRANT statement and AS/400 security rights.

TABLE 8.4

The GRANT Statement and AS/400 Security Rights

Authority	Rights							
ALL	*OBJALTER	*OBJMGT	*OBJOPR	*OBJREF	*ADD	*DLT	*READ	*UPD
ALTER	*OBJALTER							
DELETE			*OBJOPR			*DLT		
INDEX	*OBJALTER							
INSERT			*OBJOPR		*ADD			
REFERENCES				*OBJREF				
SELECT			*OBJOPR				*READ	
UPDATE			*OBJOPR					
WITH GRANT OPTION		*OBJMGT						

The LABEL ON Statement

The LABEL ON statement lets you attach descriptive text to an SQL file, view, package, or an AS/400 physical file. You also can place column headings on fields within any file. The LABEL ON statement is different from the COMMENT ON statement. LABEL ON actually updates the AS/400 object, whereas COMMENT ON updates only the SQL catalog files.

The syntax of the LABEL ON statement is

```
LABEL ON {TABLE file name |
          ALIAS  alias name |
          COLUMN file name.field name |
          PACKAGE package name} [TEXT] IS string
```

or

```
LABEL ON  file name (field name [TEXT] IS string [, ...])
```

1. `LABEL ON TABLE CATALOG IS 'Catalog Master File'`

2.  ```
    LABEL ON CATALOG
        (CATLG# IS 'Catalog Number',
         CATDSC IS 'Description',
         CATDTE IS 'Date Entered',
         CTGRY# IS 'Category Number',
         CURYR$ IS 'Sales Current Year',
         YR1$ IS 'Sales 1year ago',
         YR2$ IS 'Sales 2years ago',
         ONHAND IS 'Quantity Onhand',
         CPRICE IS 'Current Price',
         FPRICE IS 'Future Price',
         PRCDTE IS 'Date Price Effective',
         SUB# IS 'Substitute Catalog Number')
    ```

For a file, the text is placed as object text in the file name. For a field, the text serves as a column heading for the field. If a field already has text associated
    ```

with it, the field text is not changed by the LABEL ON statement; only the column headings are affected.

Because the LABEL ON statement does not require the use of SQL catalog files, you can execute it over any file on the AS/400 even if SQL did not create the file. The text cannot exceed 50 characters for a file and 60 characters for a field.

If you want to associate text with a file, you must use the first form of the LABEL ON statement. If you use the first form of the statement for a field, you can only add column headings to one field at a time.

If you use the second form of the statement, you can add column headings for as many fields as you wish. The second form is valid only for fields.

The LOCK TABLE Statement

The LOCK TABLE statement lets you specify special locking attributes for a designated file. You must have authority to the file to specify a locking operation. Using the LOCK TABLE statement is the same as using the ALCOBJ (Allocated Object) command.

The syntax of this statement is

```
LOCK TABLE file name IN {SHARE MODE | EXCLUSIVE MODE ALLOW
READ | EXCLUSIVE MODE}
```

1. This statement places an exclusive lock on the catalog master file. No one else can access this file until you end the lock either by ending the job or by issuing the DLCOBJ command.

```
LOCK TABLE CATALOG IN EXCLUSIVE MODE
```

IN SHARE MODE specifies a locking state of *SHRNUP (share no update). Only the job that holds the lock can perform any update operation. Others can read the file, but they cannot update it.

IN EXCLUSIVE MODE specifies a locking state of *EXCL (exclusive). Only the job that holds the lock can perform any operations against the file — no one else can access the file.

IN EXCLUSIVE MODE ALLOW READ specifies a locking state of *EXCLRD (exclusive read). Only the job that holds the lock can perform any operation against the file. Other jobs can only read data from the file.

When you issue the LOCK TABLE command, that locking state will remain in effect until either the job ends or you issue the DLCOBJ (Deallocate Object) command. No SQL statement exists to let you release the lock.

The RENAME Statement

The RENAME statement renames a table, a view, or an index to another name. Using this statement is the same as issuing the RNMOBJ (Rename Object) command. When you rename a table or view, you can specify the keyword TABLE. When you rename an index, you must specify the INDEX keyword. The syntax of the RENAME statement is

```
RENAME [TABLE | INDEX] file name
                TO {name [FOR SYSTEM NAME system name] |
                    SYSTEM NAME system name}
```

1. The following example of the RENAME statement renames the CATALOG file to OLDCATALOG:

```
RENAME TABLE CATALOG TO SYSTEM NAME OLDCATALOG
```

You can specify the new name of the object in the TO subclause in one of two ways. First, you can specify a new name for the object. If this name does not meet AS/400 naming conventions, you must specify a valid AS/400 name using the FOR SYSTEM NAME keyword. Second, you can give a valid AS/400 name by using the SYSTEM NAME clause. In this case, the name of the object is the same for both the database and the AS/400.

The REVOKE Statement

The REVOKE statement lets you remove AS/400 security rights from a file. Using the REVOKE statement is similar to using the RVKOBJAUT (Revoke Object Authority) command. The syntax of the REVOKE statement is

```
REVOKE {ALL [PRIVILEGES] |
            {{ALTER | DELETE | INDEX | INSERT |
              REFERENCES | SELECT | UPDATE},...}}
            ON [TABLE] {file name,...}
            FROM {PUBLIC | user profile,...}
```

1. This statement revokes ALL rights for user profile USER1 from the catalog master file:

```
REVOKE ALL ON CATALOG FROM USER1
```

You can specify any number of files from which to revoke authority by naming those files in the ON clause of this statement. The FROM clause names the users whose authority will be revoked. You can revoke authority from PUBLIC or from any number of user profiles on the system. You cannot specify PUBLIC and a user profile at the same time. Likewise, you cannot specify ALL and use any of the other rights.

If you list specific rights, you can list the authorities to revoke. The authority required to remove rights from the file on the system is the same as it is anywhere else on the AS/400.

Chapter 9

Distributive Databases and Commitment Control

In this chapter, we discuss distributive databases and commitment control — each an important part of SQL and the AS/400.

DISTRIBUTIVE DATABASES

The concept of distributive databases refers to data files residing on multiple computer systems. When we discuss distributive databases, we can talk about two distinct types of distribution. In the first type, related files may reside on different computer systems, but any individual file resides on only a single system.

With the second type of distribution, known as a multiple-system database, data for a single file is distributed over more than one computer system. A multiple-system database requires that your AS/400 have the DB2 Multisystem for OS/400 product installed. We don't explain here how to configure this type of environment; we simply discuss the SQL statements and how they relate to a multisystem environment.

Servers

SQL uses the term *server* to indicate a specific database residing on a specific computer system. The server can be either the local computer system to which you are logged on or another computer to which you have access through some type of communications network. When you are working with a specific database server, you are said to be *connected* to or have a *connection* with that server.

The computer to which you connect must support Distributed Relational Database Architecture (DRDA), which is how the AS/400 works with remote databases. Remote databases are defined to your AS/400 by means of Remote Database entries. The AS/400 commands that relate to remote database entries are found on the CMDRDB menu, which you can display by typing GO CMDRDB.

Activation Groups

The AS/400's Integrated Language Environment (ILE) lets you partition job resources (e.g., file overrides, commitment definitions, and open files) into unique units of work, called *activation groups*, for each job. Each unit of work is considered separate so that it can do work without interfering with the other units of work. A job running on the AS/400 may be part of several activation groups. Your system design determines which activation groups the job will use.

Each activation group in a job can have many connections defined for the group. However, only one connection is in use at a time for a given group. You use the SET CONNECTION statement to define the current connection to use when more than one CONNECT statement has been issued for an activation group.

Node Groups

When you are using the DB2 Multisystem for OS/400 product, you can define multiple AS/400 systems (up to 32) to look like a single database, referred to as a *node group*. Each AS/400 within this group is known as a node, and a specific AS/400 can be defined in any number of node groups.

When you define a table in this environment, records in a table will be distributed among the computers in the node group. This means that record 1 could be on one computer, record 2 on a different computer, and so on. The method for determining which records go on which computers is called *partitioning*.

Partitioning occurs by means of a partition number, which is a value from 0 – 1023. Each partition number is assigned to a node in the node group. Each node can be assigned many partition numbers. The relationship between nodes and partition numbers is stored in a partition map. The partition map is also stored as part of the node group object.

You can provide the partition map when you create a node group; otherwise, the system will generate a default map. You define a partition map by using a partitioning file, which is a physical file that defines a node number for each partition number.

When you create a distributive file, you assign that file a partitioning key. A partitioning key consists of one or more fields in the file that is being distributed. The partitioning key uses a technique called *hashing* to determine in which node in the node group the row is to be placed. Hashing is an operating-system function that takes the value of the partitioning key for a record and maps it to a partition number. The node corresponding to that partition number stores the record.

DISTRIBUTIVE DATABASE STATEMENTS

Several SQL statements relate directly to distributive database processing. These statements manage the connection of your system to a remote database.

The CONNECT Statement

The CONNECT statement sets the current activation group to point at another database server so that you can execute SQL statements against a database on that server. The database server names must be defined to the current AS/400 in the remote database directory. After you successfully connect to a remote database, the SQL statements you execute will affect data on the specified server.

The syntax of the CONNECT statement is

```
CONNECT [RESET |
    TO server [USER user profile USING password]]
```

1. This statement connects you to the database on the server named PRO-
    DUCTION.

    ```
    CONNECT PRODUCTION
    ```

Two different types of connections can be made — a *distributive unit of
work* (DUW) and a *remote unit of work* (RUW). With DUW, the default, you
can have more than one connection defined to your activation group. If you
issue more than one CONNECT, you must use the SET CONNECTION statement to define which is the current connection.

With RUW, when a second CONNECT statement is issued, the first connection is disconnected before the new connection is made.

If you do not specify any arguments, the CONNECT statement returns information about the current connection status, but no actual connection is made.

CONNECT RESET returns the operating environment to the local server.

Using the TO clause, you can specify the name of the server to which a
connection is requested. You can optionally specify a user profile and pass-
word when you attempt to make the connection.

The DISCONNECT Statement

The DISCONNECT statement ends one or more connections defined for an
activation group. The syntax of the DISCONNECT statement is

```
DISCONNECT {server name | CURRENT | ALL [SQL]}
```

You can specify the name of the server to end, the CURRENT connection, or
ALL connections.

1. This statement initiates a disconnect from the server named PRODUCTION.

    ```
    DISCONNECT PRODUCTION
    ```

The RELEASE Statement

The RELEASE statement, used in conjunction with commitment control, places
one or more connections into a release-pending state. The RELEASE statement
indicates that when the next commit operation is performed, the identified connections will be ended. We discuss commitment control in the next section.

The syntax of the RELEASE statement is

```
RELEASE {server name | CURRENT | ALL [SQL]}
```

1. This statement places the connection to PRODUCTION in a release-pending
    state until the next commit operation.

    ```
    RELEASE PRODUCTION
    ```

The SET CONNECTION Statement

The SET CONNECTION statement sets the identified connection as the current connection for the activation group. The syntax of the SET CONNECTION statement is

```
SET CONNECTION server name
```

The server name specified must already have been defined by the CONNECT statement.

1. This statement establishes the connection to PRODUCTION as the current connection.

```
SET CONNECTION PRODUCTION
```

COMMITMENT CONTROL

Commitment control refers to a method you can use to designate that changes be made to database files, but the changes won't be implemented until your application *commits* them to the database. This approach, used with complex transactions that span several database files, ensures that every file is updated properly based on the application design; it also lets an application *roll back*, or not apply, the changes to a database file. Consequently, commitment control supports data integrity in a database.

Journaling

For commitment control to work, the database files in question must be journaled. When you create an SQL collection via the CREATE COLLECTION statement, the journal and journal receivers are created automatically. When you create a table (CREATE TABLE) in this collection, the table is automatically added to the journal.

Once a file has been journaled, any changes made to that file are automatically entered into the journal receiver, which serves as an audit of changes that were made to the file.

Commit and Rollback Concepts

When a database is journaled, you can design an application to ensure the integrity of the database through application programming. To understand this concept, you must think in terms of a *transaction unit*. A transaction unit consists of any changes made to a database between a fixed point in time, called a *point of consistency*, and a commit. Each commitment boundary is considered a point of consistency. Changes made between points of consistency are considered the transaction unit. These changes are not applied to the database until either a COMMIT statement or a ROLLBACK statement is issued. You can make any number of adds and changes to any number of files during a transaction unit.

A COMMIT statement instructs the computer to apply the changes made as permanent. A ROLLBACK statement backs out the changes made during the transaction unit.

Isolation Level

The isolation level is the degree to which an activation group is isolated from other concurrently executing activation groups. Any of the following five specific isolation levels can be in effect for an activation group:

- **Repeatable Read (RR) isolation level** — Any record read during a transaction unit is not changed by other activation groups. This activation group cannot read any changes made by other activation groups until the record has been committed.

- **Read Stability (RS) isolation level** — Similar to the RR isolation level, except that the RS isolation level does not completely isolate the activation group from other activation groups. One possible result at the RS level is that additional records, called *phantom records*, will appear when the same query is issued more than once.

- **Cursor Stability (CS) isolation level** — Similar to the RR and RS isolation levels, except that the CS isolation level only ensures that the current record of an updated cursor is not changed by other activation groups.

- **Uncommitted Read (UR) isolation level** — Any record read during a unit of work can be changed by other activation groups. This activation group can read any record changed by another activation group even if that change has not been committed to the database.

- **No Commit (NC) isolation level** — Commit and rollback operations have no effect when you specify this isolation level. All database changes apply at the time they are issued.

COMMITMENT CONTROL STATEMENTS

To help you manage commitment control, SQL includes the following commitment control statements.

The COMMIT Statement

The COMMIT statement ends a transaction unit and applies all database changes made during that transaction unit. The syntax of the COMMIT statement is

```
COMMIT [WORK][HOLD]
```

The COMMIT WORK statement is the same as the COMMIT statement. You use the COMMIT HOLD statement to place a hold on resources used during a transaction unit; current open cursors are not closed and prepared SQL statements are preserved (we discuss cursors and prepared SQL statements in Chapter 10).

The ROLLBACK Statement

The ROLLBACK statement ends a transaction unit and backs out any changes made to the database during the transaction unit. The rollback is done to the previous point of consistency (commitment boundary). The syntax of the ROLLBACK statement is

```
ROLLBACK [WORK][HOLD]
```

The ROLLBACK WORK statement is the same as the ROLLBACK statement. You use the ROLLBACK HOLD statement to place a hold on resources used during a transaction unit; current open cursors are not closed and prepared SQL statements are preserved (we discuss cursors and prepared SQL statements in Chapter 10).

The SET TRANSACTION Statement

You use the SET TRANSACTION statement to set the isolation level for SQL statements for the current activation group. This statement must first be executed during a transaction unit. You cannot specify this statement if the current connection is to a remote application server.

The syntax of the SET TRANSACTION statement is

```
SET TRANSACTION  ISOLATION LEVEL
{NO COMMIT | NC | NONE |
                 READ UNCOMMITTED, READ WRITE  | UR | CHG |
                 READ COMMITED  | CS |
                 REPEATABLE READ  | RS | ALL |
                 SERIALIZABLE | RR}
```

1. These statements place the current isolation level to no commit.

```
SET TRANSACTION ISOLATION LEVEL  NO COMMIT
SET TRANSACTION ISOLATION LEVEL  NC
```

2. These statements place the current isolation level to cursor stability.

```
SET TRANSACTION ISOLATION LEVEL  READ COMMITED
SET TRANSACTION ISOLATION LEVEL  CS
```

The SELECT, UPDATE, DELETE, and INSERT Statements

The NO COMMIT, NC, or NONE statements specify an isolation level of NC. The READ UNCOMMITED, READ WRITE, UR, or CHG statements specify an isolation level of UR. The READ COMMITED or CS statements specify an isolation level of CS. The REPEATABLE READ, RS, or ALL statements specify an isolation level of RS. The SERIALIZABLE or RR statements specify an isolation level of RR.

When you work with the SELECT, UPDATE, DELETE, and INSERT statements, you can use the optional WITH clause to specify the isolation level to be used when the statement is executed. The WITH clause only affects the isolation level during the execution of the statement; it does not change the isolation level of the current activation group.

For the SELECT statement, you specify the WITH clause after the ORDER BY clause. For the UPDATE statement, you specify the WITH clause after the WHERE clause. For the INSERT statement, you specify the WITH clause after the VALUES clause or the SELECT statement. For the DELETE statement, you specify the WITH clause after the WHERE clause.

The syntax of the WITH clause is the same for all four statements:

```
WITH {NC | UR | CS | RS | RR}
```

Chapter 10

Embedded SQL Concepts

When you purchase SQL/400, you acquire the capability to embed SQL statements within an HLL program. In this chapter, we discuss the concepts you must understand to write embedded SQL programs. We only discuss the concepts as they relate to ILE RPG, with a little RPG/400 thrown in. We will provide the syntax and rules for the SQL statements in Chapter 11.

SOURCE ENTRY AND COMPILATION

Let's look first at how you enter SQL statements within the HLL program and then at how you compile those statements.

When you create a source member for embedded SQL, you must specify the correct source member type. For RPG/400, the source type is SQLRPG; for ILE RPG, the source type is SQLRPGLE. The command to create the SQL program is CRTSQLRPG for RPG/400 and CRTSQLRPGI for ILE RPG.

You place SQL statements within your HLL program source by means of the "begin" and "end" SQL delimiters. In RPG, you do this in the calculation specifications, using this format:

```
C/EXEC SQL
C+    . . .
C/END-EXEC
```

The beginning delimiter is C/EXEC SQL. The beginning characters in each line of the SQL statement are C+. The ending delimiter is C/END-EXEC. For example,

```
C/EXEC SQL
C+    SELECT FIELD1 INTO :VAR1
C+       FROM FILEA
C+     WHERE FIELD2 = '14'
C/END-EXEC
C/EXEC SQL  EXECUTE IMMEDIATE UPDATE CATALOG  SET YR1$=0
C/END-EXEC
```

Both of these examples are valid.

You can place comments within the SQL statement by placing an * in position 7 of the calculation specification. For example,

```
C/EXEC SQL
C*   Get field for record 14
C+       SELECT FIELD1 INTO :VAR
C+          FROM FILEA
C+         WHERE FIELD2 = '14'
C/END-EXEC
```

An embedded SQL program goes through two distinct steps when it is compiled. The first step is a precompile. The precompile step takes the SQL statements in the HLL source and builds the constructs needed to execute the SQL statements. The precompile step creates a work source member and performs many validations of the SQL statements entered in the program. If the precompiler detects any errors, the second step is not performed. The second step compiles the work member and creates the actual program object.

When you compile an embedded SQL program, you receive two spool files — the first for the precompile step, the second for the actual compile.

If you are not using commitment control, you will need to remember to specify COMIT(*NONE) on the CRTSQL command if your HLL program uses the UPDATE, DELETE, or INSERT statement. If you fail to do this, the SQL statements will not execute because SQL expects commitment control to be active. This is the most common mistake when creating embedded SQL programs.

PACKAGES

An SQL package is a special object that contains information about a distributive SQL embedded program. A distributive SQL program is defined whenever the program is bound to a remote database — that is, when you specify the relational database name (RDB parameter) on a CRTSQLxxx (Create SQL) command. You can also create packages using the CRTSQLPKG (Create SQL Package) command.

The name of the package is defined in the SQLPKG parameter. The package will have an object type of *SQLPKG. The actual package is created on the system specified by the RDB parameter.

When a distributed SQL program is created, the name of the SQL package and an internal identifier are saved in the program. These identifiers are used at runtime to find the SQL package and to verify that the SQL package is correct for this program. Because the name of the SQL package is critical for running distributed SQL programs, you cannot move, rename, or duplicate an SQL package, or restore it to a different library.

You can delete an SQL package by using the DLTSQLPKG (Delete SQL Package) command. This command deletes an SQL package on the local system only; to delete the package at the remote server, you must log on to that server and delete the object.

ERROR HANDLING

You can address error handling within an HLL program for SQL statements by either of two methods. The first method uses the SQLCA communications area field SQLCOD (for more information, see Appendix B). The second method uses the WHENEVER statement.

Monitoring for errors is important because if an SQL statement fails to execute, your HLL program will continue processing; the only way to know whether the statement failed is to check the error code or to use the WHENEVER statement. It is not enough to get the program running and then assume it will always execute that SQL statement correctly, because conditions can exist outside your program that can cause the SQL statement to fail. For example, if a database field changes in size or attribute, you will not receive a level check when the HLL program is called.

The SQLCOD Method

SQLCOD is a numeric field within the SQLCA communications area that is updated every time an SQL statement is executed. This field has one of the following values:

Negative	Statement failed.
0	Statement executed correctly.
100	End of file occurred.
Positive	Statement executed correctly; however, warnings have been generated.

Within your HLL program, you can test the SQLCOD field to see what the results of any SQL statement might be. This test is extremely useful when you are building dynamic SQL statements that may or may not have a correct syntax.

The WHENEVER Method

The WHENEVER statement acts as a global message monitor. When your system generates a message about an SQL statement, the WHENEVER statement dictates the action to take.

You can test for three different conditions using the WHENEVER statement: SQLERROR, SQLWARNING, and NOT FOUND. Testing for each of these conditions is equivalent to testing the SQLCOD field for a value. For example, the SQLERROR condition is the same as SQLCOD being negative, the SQLWARNING condition is the same as SQLCOD being greater than 0 but less than 100, and the NOT FOUND condition is the same as SQLCOD having a value of 100.

Next, you can either indicate that processing is to continue as normal or that it is to branch to a specific point in the program (in RPG, this branch point is a TAG opcode).

USING HOST VARIABLES

When you write an application program using embedded SQL, the chances are you will want to pass information back and forth between your program and the SQL statements. You do this by using host variables. Host variables are nothing more than the standard field names you use in your HLL program; however, you reference those names within an SQL statement by defining the variable with a colon (:) immediately followed by the name of the field (e.g., :VAR1).

Using host variables eliminates the need for your program to use hard-coded values. Many statements allow for a host variable somewhere within the statement. Table 10.1 represents some of the SQL statements that allow host variables; this list does not include those statements we discuss in Chapter 11. In addition, any SQL built-in function can contain a host variable name.

TABLE 10.1
Some SQL Statements That Allow Host Variables

SQL Statement	Parameter	What Host Variable Contains
CONNECT	TO clause	Server name
	USER clause	User profile
	USING clause	Password
DELETE	WHERE clause	Value on the right hand side of a conditional test
DISCONNECT		Server name
INSERT	VALUES clause	Value to load into table
RELEASE		Server name
SET CONNECTION		Server name
UPDATE	SET clause	Value on the right hand side of the assignment
	WHERE clause	Value on the right hand side of a conditional test

When you use host variables, it is your responsibility to ensure that the data types between the database and your program are correct.

```
1. C/EXEC SQL
   C+    UPDATE CATALOG
   C+        SET FPRICE = CPRICE * :INCRAT
   C/END-EXEC
```

Host Structures
When you talk about a host variable, you can reference either a single host variable or many variables at one time. When you reference many variables, you will use what is called a *host structure*.

You often use host structures when you retrieve data from a database file, such as in the SELECT INTO or FETCH statements. You reference a host structure in the same way you do a single variable. The difference is that with a host structure you specify the name of the structure instead of a single host variable.

In RPG, a host structure is a data structure. The layout of the structure must match the fields for which you are mapping.

```
1. D DS1              DS
   D  SUMQTY                 1    11  0
   D  SUMAMT                12    22  2

   C/EXEC SQL
   C+    SELECT DECIMAL(SUM(SHPQTY),11,0),
   C+           DECIMAL(SUM(AMOUNT),11,2)  INTO :DS1
```

```
C+        FROM SALESHST A INNER JOIN CATALOG B
C+              ON A.CATLG# = B.CATLG#
C+        WHERE CTGRY# = :SELCT#
C/END-EXEC
```

Host Structure Arrays

You may have a situation where you are reading many records or building a
group of records within your HLL program and you want to reference that
group of records at the same time. You do this by using what is called a *host
structure array.* In RPG, a host structure array is a multiple-occurrence data
structure, with each occurrence being a single record or row. You use a host
structure array with a multiple-row FETCH or a blocked INSERT statement.

A good example of where you might use a host structure array is with a
procedure that is called from an ODBC client. The procedure generates what
is called a *result set,* which is sent back to the client. To build the result set
within your HLL program, you use a host structure array.

1. This example uses a host structure array. The code is not complete, but it
   demonstrates what the host-structure coding might look like.

```
D DS2            DS                  OCCURS(10)
D   CATLG#               1     20
D   SUMQTY              21     31  0
D   SUMAMT              32     42  2

C/EXEC SQL
C+  DECLARE CURSOR C1 FOR
C+    SELECT A.CATLG#,DECIMAL(SUM(SHPQTY),11,0),
C+           DECIMAL(SUM(AMOUNT),11,2)
C+      FROM SALESHST A INNER JOIN CATALOG B
C+            ON A.CATLG# = B.CATLG#
C+      WHERE CTGRY# = :SELCT#
C+      GROUP BY A.CATLG#
C/END-EXEC

C/EXEC SQL
C+      FETCH C1 INTO :DS2 FOR 10 ROWS
C/END EXEC
```

Indicator Variables

When you retrieve a database field and that field can contain null values, your
HLL program needs to know this. You notify the HLL program by using what
is called an *indicator variable.*

The indicator variable is a half-word integer variable, which means the
variable is defined as a binary number with a length of 2 or 4. You reference
an indicator variable immediately after the host variable. You separate the host
variable from the indicator variable with a colon (:) (e.g., :HOSTV1:INDV1). In
this example, the host variable is HOSTV1; the indicator variable is INDV1.

If a database field contains a null value at the time it is passed to your HLL program, the indicator variable associated with that field will be set to a value of -1. You can then test within your HLL program to determine whether a null value exists in the database field. If you don't specify an indicator variable and the database field contains a null value, the SQLCOD field in the SQLCA communications area will be set to a negative value.

You also can use indicator variables to set the value of a database field to null when a record is updated. In this case, you set the indicator variable to a value of -1 and then update the database record. This sets the database field to a null value.

In addition to using indicator variables for null-value processing, you can use them to inform your program when data-mapping errors occur for a field or when a string value has been truncated. If a data-mapping error occurs, the indicator variable will be set to a value of -2. If string truncation occurs, the indicator variable will be set to a value equal to the length of the original string value.

One last note about indicator variables: If, within an SQL statement, you wish to test whether a database field contains a null value, you do not use an indicator variable; instead, you use the IS NULL expression.

1. This is an example using an indicator variable.

```
C/EXEC SQL
C+     SELECT CATLG#,CPRICE,FPRICE
C+       INTO :CATLG#,:CPRICE,:FPRICE:FNULL
C+       FROM CATALOG
C+      WHERE CATLG# = :SEL#
C/END-EXEC
```

Indicator Structure

When you use a host structure to retrieve database fields and you want to use indicator variables for those fields, you need to set up an indicator structure, in which every indicator variable is mapped to every host variable. In RPG, an indicator structure is a data structure.

1. This is an example of a host structure and an indicator structure.

```
D DS1             DS
D   CATLG#                   1      20
D   CPRICE                  21      27  2
D   FPRICE                  28      34  2

D IN1             DS
D   IND1                     1      4B 0
D   IND2                     5      8B 0
D   IND3                     9     12B 0

C/EXEC SQL
C+     SELECT CATLG#,CPRICE,FPRICE
C+       INTO :DS1:IN1
C+       FROM CATALOG
```

```
C+      WHERE CATLG# = :SEL#
C/END-EXEC
```

READING A FILE

With embedded SQL, a typical application program retrieves information from a database and processes that information within your program. This action requires the program to read the file, using one of two methods. The first method uses the SELECT INTO statement; the second uses the FETCH statement with a cursor.

The SELECT INTO Method

The SELECT INTO method for reading a file is simple to use and understand. With this statement, you can retrieve a single record (and only one record) from a database file and load the results into host variables.

```
1. C/EXEC SQL
   C+      SELECT COUNT(*) INTO :COUNT
   C+         FROM CATALOG
   C+         WHERE CTGRY# = :SELCAT
   C/END-EXEC

2. C/EXEC SQL
   C+      SELECT CATLG#, CATDSC, CTGRY#
   C+         INTO :CATLG#,:CATDSC,:CTGRY#
   C+         FROM CATALOG
   C+      WHERE CATLG# = :SELCAT
   C/END-EXEC
```

The DECLARE CURSOR/OPEN/FETCH/CLOSE Method

The second method for retrieving records is to use the FETCH statement with a cursor. You can think of a cursor as an Open Data Path (ODP) on the AS/400. To use a cursor, follow these steps:

1. Declare the cursor. You declare the cursor using the DECLARE CURSOR statement. This statement actually contains the SELECT statement to be executed. You can either hard-code the SELECT statement within the DECLARE CURSOR statement or you can prepare it from a string value (we discuss prepared statements later in this chapter).

```
C/EXEC SQL
C+      DECLARE C1 CURSOR FOR
C+         SELECT * FROM CATALOG
C/END-EXEC
```

2. Open the cursor. Open the cursor via the OPEN statement. Opening the cursor is what actually executes the SELECT statement; however, records are not passed to your HLL program until the FETCH statement is executed.

```
C/EXEC SQL
C+      OPEN C1
C/END-EXEC
```

3. Fetch the records. Fetch the records using the FETCH statement. The FETCH statement returns the database fields selected into host variables for single or multiple records. In most cases, you will use the single-record retrieval method.

```
C/EXEC SQL
C+      FETCH C1 INTO :DS1
C/END-EXEC
```

4. Close the cursor. Once you are done reading records, you close the cursor using the CLOSE statement.

```
C/EXEC SQL
C+      CLOSE C1
C/END-EXEC
```

Note that in this discussion we don't mention using host variables within the SELECT statement itself. If you want to do this, you must use parameter markers, which we discuss later in this chapter.

Updating a Record

When you read a record from a database file and that record can be updated, you can update or delete the record with the UPDATE or DELETE statements using the WHERE CURRENT OF clause.

When you retrieve a record and it can be updated, the record will be locked just as any other file on the AS/400 would be. To prevent locking, you can use the FOR READ ONLY clause on the SELECT statement. Doing this, however, prevents the record from ever being updated.

1. This example shows how you might update a database using a cursor.

```
C/EXEC SQL
C+      DECLARE C1 CURSOR FOR
C+      SELECT * FROM CATALOG
C+        FOR UPDATE OF FPRICE
C/END-EXEC

C/EXEC SQL
C+      OPEN C1
C/END-EXEC

C/EXEC SQL
C+      FETCH C1 INTO :DS1
C/END-EXEC

C/EXEC SQL
C+      UPDATE CATALOG
C+        SET FPRICE = CPRICE * :INCRAT
C+      WHERE CURRENT OF C1
C/END-EXEC
```

PREPARING STATEMENTS

Embedded SQL gives you the capability to prepare and execute SQL statements dynamically, which means you can design your application programs with greater flexibility.

You can prepare SQL statements in one of two ways. One method is to use the EXECUTE IMMEDIATE statement; the other is to use the PREPARE statement. Both methods require you to build a string that contains the SQL statement to be executed.

The difference between the two approaches is that EXECUTE IMMEDIATE will execute the statement right now. PREPARE will build a SQL statement that in turn lets the statement be executed many times. This means that the SQL statement is prepared only once, thus reducing the overhead required to execute that statement over and over again. If you can execute an SQL statement many times, you should use the PREPARE method.

You can use the PREPARE statement in two different ways. You can use the EXECUTE statement to run the PREPARE statement, or you can use the PREPARE statement to build a SELECT statement dynamically and then use the SELECT statement with a cursor.

You cannot execute every SQL statement dynamically; the following list includes those SQL statements that are valid:

ALTER TABLE	GRANT
CALL	INSERT
COMMENT ON	LABEL ON
COMMIT	LOCK TABLE
CREATE COLLECTION	RENAME
CREATE INDEX	REVOKE
CREATE PROCEDURE	ROLLBACK
CREATE TABLE	SELECT (Note: cannot be used within EXECUTE or EXECUTE IMMEDIATE; only used with cursors.)
CREATE VIEW	SET TRANSACTION
DELETE	UPDATE
DROP	

The EXECUTE IMMEDIATE Method

When you use the EXECUTE IMMEDIATE method to execute an SQL statement, you simply build your SQL statement into a string value, then issue the EXECUTE IMMEDIATE statement.

The EXECUTE IMMEDIATE method cannot use parameter markers within the SQL string (we explain parameter markers later in this chapter). If you need to use a parameter marker, you must use the PREPARE/EXECUTE method.

1. STRING contains a value of:
   "UPDATE CATALOG SET FPRICE = CPRICE * 1.04 WHERE CTGRY# = 15"

```
C/EXEC SQL
C+    EXECUTE IMMEDIATE  :STRING
C/END-EXEC
```

The PREPARE/EXECUTE Method

When you prepare, then execute, an SQL statement, you first issue the PREPARE statement; then you can use the EXECUTE statement as many times as you want. If you need to change the SQL statement that you prepared, you issue the PREPARE statement a second time.

If you want to use host variables within the SQL statement, you cannot reference the variables directly within the SQL statement. You reference host variables via parameter markers.

1. STRING contains a value of:
   "UPDATE CATALOG SET YR1$ = 0"

```
C/EXEC SQL
C+    PREPARE P1 FROM :STRING
C/END-EXEC

C/EXEC SQL
C+    EXECUTE P1
C/END-EXEC
```

The PREPARE with Cursor Method

This approach to using the PREPARE statement lets you build a SELECT statement dynamically within an HLL program and still use the OPEN/FETCH method to retrieve records. Again, if you wish to specify host variables within the SELECT statement, you use parameter markers.

1. STRING contains a value of:
   "SELECT * FROM CATALOG WHERE   CTGRY# = 15"

```
C/EXEC SQL
C+    PREPARE P1 FROM :STRING
C/END-EXEC

C/EXEC SQL
C+    DECLARE C1 CURSOR FOR P1
C/END-EXEC

C/EXEC SQL
C+    OPEN C1
C/END-EXEC

C/EXEC SQL
C+    FETCH C1 INTO :DS1
C/END-EXEC
```

```
C/EXEC SQL
C+      CLOSE C1
C/END-EXEC
```

PARAMETER MARKERS

When you use a prepared SQL statement, you cannot specify host variables directly within that SQL statement. You can, however, use parameter markers. Parameter markers represent a method of string substitution at the time the SQL statement is executed.

You identify a parameter marker within the SQL statement with a question mark (?). Then the EXECUTE statement or the OPEN statement specifies the USING clause, which in turn specifies the host variables to be used.

The number of host variables you reference within the USING clause must match the number of parameter markers in the SQL string. You can use either individual host variable names or you can use a host structure.

1. STRING contains a value of:

```
"SELECT * FROM CATALOG WHERE CTGRY# = ?"

C/EXEC SQL
C+      PREPARE P1 FROM :STRING
C/END-EXEC

C/EXEC SQL
C+      DECLARE C1 CURSOR FOR P1
C/END-EXEC

C/EXEC SQL
C+      OPEN C1 USING :SEL#
C/END-EXEC

C/EXEC SQL
C+      FETCH C1 INTO :DS1
C/END-EXEC
```

2. STRING contains a value of:

```
"DELETE FROM SALESHST WHERE SUBSTR(DIGITS(SHPDTE),1,2) = ?"

C/EXEC SQL
C+      PREPARE P1 FROM :STRING
C/END-EXEC

C/EXEC SQL
C+      EXECUTE P1 USING :YEAR
C/END-EXEC
```

VARIABLE FIELD SELECTION

Most times when you retrieve database fields from a file, you use what is called a *fixed list*. This means that the fields retrieved are always the same for the program. Fixed-list programming is very simple.

However, SQL provides the capability for you to dynamically specify what fields are to be retrieved during the program. This capability is known as *varying-list selection.* You cannot use varying-list programming with RPG/400 applications; however, you can use ILE RPG for this approach.

To use varying-list selection, you must use the SQL descriptor area SQLDA. The SQLDA contains the information about the host variables being used. Within the SQLDA structure is a variable called SQLVAR, which is an array of values that describe the host variables that will receive the data. Each occurrence of SQLVAR describes a single host variable.

Before you can retrieve data into the SQLDA, several variables within the SQLDA must be set properly. These variables are as follows:

- **SQLN** contains the number of occurrences of SQLVAR. You must set this number before you retrieve any data. For practical purposes, you should set this value to the estimated maximum number of fields to be retrieved. In ILE RPG, you must set the size of the **SQLVAR** array to its maximum value because the size of the array is determined at the time the program is compiled.

- **SQLDABC** indicates the length of the SQLDA. You calculate this value using the following formula: SQLN * Length of SQLVAR, which is 80 + 16. For example, SQLN=20; therefore, SQLDABC is 20* 80 + 16, or 1616.

- **SQLD** contains the number of actual occurrences being used in SQLVAR for the statement being executed. You must set this number before you retrieve any data.

When you define the SQLDA, you can either explicitly specify all of the data within your application or you can use the DESCRIBE statement to get the information about the varying-list selection.

Each occurrence of SQLVAR contains information about the host variables being referenced. The fields within this array are as follows:

- **SQLTYPE** — Specifies the data type of the host variable.

- **SQLLEN** — Specifies the length of the host variable.

- **SQLDATA** — Is a 16-byte pointer variable that specifies the address of the host variables used for the varying-list.

- **SQLIND** — Is a 16-byte pointer variable that specifies the address of the indicator variables used for the varying-list.

- **SQLNAME** — Contains the name of the field being selected.

Once you have the descriptions of the data being retrieved loaded into the SQLDA, you must set the pointers to where the data will be placed within your HLL program. You set the SQLDATA and SQLIND variables for each occurrence within SQLVAR.

Because SQLDATA and SQLIND are pointers, you must set up storage locations for the possible fields being retrieved and then assign pointer values to those locations. Once you have set the pointer values, you then load them into the SQLVAR elements.

PROGRAM4, at the end of this chapter, shows the steps necessary to perform varying-list selection within ILE RPG.

EXAMPLE PROGRAMS

The following example programs use the embedded SQL techniques described in this chapter.

PROGRAM1

This program deletes records from the SALESHST file where the date is less than or equal to a given year. The year is passed as a parameter to the program.

```
FQPRINT   O   F  132       PRINTER
C     *ENTRY       PLIST
C                  PARM                 YEAR          2
C                  Z-ADD   0            COUNT1        5 0
C                  Z-ADD   0            COUNT2        5 0
 *
 *  Get count of number of records that will be deleted
 *
C/exec sql
C+      SELECT COUNT(*) INTO :COUNT1
C+         FROM SALESHST
C+        WHERE SUBSTR(DIGITS(SHPDTE),1,2) <= :YEAR
C/end-exec
 *
 *  Delete records
 *
C/exec sql
C+      DELETE FROM SALESHST
C+        WHERE SUBSTR(DIGITS(SHPDTE),1,2) <= :YEAR
C/end-exec
 *
 *  Verify that all records got deleted
 *
C/exec sql
C+      SELECT COUNT(*) INTO :COUNT2
C+         FROM SALESHST
C+        WHERE SUBSTR(DIGITS(SHPDTE),1,2) <= :YEAR
C/end-exec
C                  EXCEPT   LINE1
C     COUNT2       IFNE     0
C                  EXCEPT   LINE2
C                  ENDIF
C                  MOVE    *ON        *INLR
OQPRINT   E          LINE1        2
O                    COUNT1       4   19
O                                     35 'RECORDS DELETED'
O         E          LINE2        1
```

```
O                                        8 '*ERROR*'
O                        COUNT2      4  19
O                                       39 'RECORDS NOT DELETED'
```

PROGRAM2

PROGRAM2 lists the contents of the CATALOG master file. This program
demonstrates a cursor using static field selection.

```
FQPRINT    O    F 132        PRINTER
D DS1           E DS                  EXTNAME(CATALOG)
 *
 *   Declare SELECT statement
 *
C/exec sql
C+     DECLARE C1 CURSOR FOR
C+       SELECT *
C+         FROM CATALOG
C+         ORDER BY CTGRY#, CATLG#
C/end-exec
 *
 *   Open cursor
 *
C/exec sql
C+        OPEN C1
C/end-exec
 *
 *   Read through file until EOF
 *
C       SQLCOD      DOUEQ      100
C/exec sql
C+       FETCH C1 INTO :DS1
C/end-exec
C       SQLCOD      IFNE       100
C                   EXCEPT    LINE1
C                   ENDIF
 *
C                   ENDDO
 *
 *   Close the cursor
 *
C/exec sql
C+        CLOSE C1
C/end-exec
C                   MOVE       *ON          *INLR
OQPRINT    E            LINE1         1
O                       CTGRY#      4    5
O                       CATLG#          27
O                       CATDSC          70
O                       CPRICE      4   85
```

PROGRAM3

This program is the same as PROGRAM2, except that the sort sequence is
determined by a parameter being passed into the program. This program represents building an SQL statement and then processing that statement.

```
FQPRINT    O   F  132        PRINTER
D DS1          E DS                   EXTNAME(CATALOG)
D STRING         S           100A
D STMT1          C                    CONST('SELECT * FROM CATALOG')
D ORDER1         C                    CONST('ORDER BY CTGRY#,CATLG#')
D ORDER2         C                    CONST('ORDER BY CATLG#')
D ORDER3         C                    CONST('ORDER BY CPRICE DESC,-
D                                     CATLG#')
D ORDER4         C                    CONST('ORDER BY CATDSC')
C     *ENTRY      PLIST
C                 PARM                SORT            1
 *
 *   Build SELECT string to execute
 *
C                 SELECT
C     SORT        WHENEQ   '1'
C     STMT1       CAT      ORDER1:1   STRING
C     SORT        WHENEQ   '2'
C     STMT1       CAT      ORDER2:1   STRING
C     SORT        WHENEQ   '3'
C     STMT1       CAT      ORDER3:1   STRING
C     SORT        WHENEQ   '4'
C     STMT1       CAT      ORDER4:1   STRING
C                 ENDSL
 *
 *   Prepare statement
 *
C/exec sql
C+      PREPARE P1 FROM :STRING
C/end-exec
 *
 *   Declare Cursor
 *
C/exec sql
C+      DECLARE C1 CURSOR FOR P1
C/end-exec
 *
 *   Open cursor
 *
C/exec sql
C+       OPEN C1
C/end-exec
 *
 *   Read through file until EOF
 *
C     SQLCOD      DOUEQ    100
C/exec sql
C+       FETCH C1 INTO :DS1
C/end-exec
C     SQLCOD      IFNE     100
C                 EXCEPT   LINE1
```

```
C                    ENDIF
 *
C                    ENDDO
 *
 *   Close the cursor
 *
C/exec sql
C+         CLOSE C1
C/end-exec
C                    MOVE      *ON           *INLR
OQPRINT     E              LINE1        1
O                           CTGRY#       4      5
O                           CATLG#             27
O                           CATDSC             70
O                           CPRICE       4     85
```

PROGRAM4

This program extracts specified fields from the CATALOG file and prints them.
This program is an example of varying-list selection. This program does not
attempt to make the output "pretty"; it merely provides a fast dump of the
data. Obviously, if you were to write this type of program, you would put
more effort into formatting the data.

```
FQPRINT    O    F   132         PRINTER
D CATLG#          S              20A
D CATDSC          S              40A
D CATDTE          S               6S 0
D CTGRY#          S               3P 0
D CURYR$          S               7P 2
D YR1$            S               7P 2
D YR2$            S               7P 2
D ONHAND          S               7P 0
D CPRICE          S               7P 2
D FPRICE          S               7P 2
D PRCDTE          S               6S 0
D SUB#            S              20A
D WORK            S              40
D WORK#           S               6S 0
D WORK#1          S               3P 0
D WORK#2          S               7P 0
D WORK#3          S               7P 2
D #DEC            S               1B 0
D #DIG            S               1B 0
D COMMA           S               1
D LINLEN          S               5P 0
D POTLEN          S               5P 0
D PRTLN1          S             132A
D PRTLN2          S             132A
D PTR             S               *   DIM(12)
D SELFLD          DS
D  ARR                     1     72   DIM(12)
D STRING          S             200A
D STMT1           C                   CONST('SELECT')
D STMT2           C                   CONST('FROM CATALOG')
D SQL_NUM         C                   12
```

```
C       *ENTRY        PLIST
C                     PARM                    SELFLD        72
 *
 *   Include SQL descriptor area
 *
C/exec sql
C+      INCLUDE SQLDA
C/end-exec
 *
 *   Build field list to select
 *
C                     EVAL      STRING = STMT1
 *
C       1             DO        12          IX              3 0
C       ARR(IX)       IFNE      *BLANKS
C       STRING        CAT       COMMA:0       STRING
C       STRING        CAT       ARR(IX):1     STRING
C                     EVAL      COMMA = ','
C                     ENDIF
C                     ENDDO
 *
C       STRING        CAT       STMT2:1       STRING
 *
 *   Get pointers to data field storage areas
 *
C       1             DO        12          IX
C       ARR(IX)       IFNE      *BLANKS
C                     SELECT
C       ARR(IX)       WHENEQ    'CATLG#'
C                     EVAL      PTR(IX) = %ADDR(CATLG#)
C       ARR(IX)       WHENEQ    'CATDSC'
C                     EVAL      PTR(IX) = %ADDR(CATDSC)
C       ARR(IX)       WHENEQ    'CATDTE'
C                     EVAL      PTR(IX) = %ADDR(CATDTE)
C       ARR(IX)       WHENEQ    'CTGRY#'
C                     EVAL      PTR(IX) = %ADDR(CTGRY#)
C       ARR(IX)       WHENEQ    'CURYR$'
C                     EVAL      PTR(IX) = %ADDR(CURYR$)
C       ARR(IX)       WHENEQ    'YR1$'
C                     EVAL      PTR(IX) = %ADDR(YR1$)
C       ARR(IX)       WHENEQ    'YR2$'
C                     EVAL      PTR(IX) = %ADDR(YR2$)
C       ARR(IX)       WHENEQ    'ONHAND'
C                     EVAL      PTR(IX) = %ADDR(ONHAND)
C       ARR(IX)       WHENEQ    'CPRICE'
C                     EVAL      PTR(IX) = %ADDR(CPRICE)
C       ARR(IX)       WHENEQ    'FPRICE'
C                     EVAL      PTR(IX) = %ADDR(FPRICE)
C       ARR(IX)       WHENEQ    'PRCDTE'
C                     EVAL      PTR(IX) = %ADDR(PRCDTE)
C       ARR(IX)       WHENEQ    'SUB#'
C                     EVAL      PTR(IX) = %ADDR(SUB#)
C                     ENDSL
C                     ENDIF
C                     ENDDO
 *
 *   Prepare statement
```

```
 *
C/exec sql
C+     PREPARE P1 FROM :STRING
C/end-exec
 *
 *  Get SQLDA information about selected fields
 *
C                     EVAL      SQLN = 12
C/exec sql
C+     DESCRIBE P1 INTO :SQLDA
C/end-exec
 *
 *  Load pointer addresses
 *
C    1             DO        12            IX
C    ARR(IX)       IFNE      *BLANKS
C                  EVAL      SQLVAR = SQL_VAR(IX)
C                  EVAL      SQLDATA = PTR(IX)
C                  EVAL      SQL_VAR(IX) = SQLVAR
C                  ENDIF
C                  ENDDO
 *
 *  Declare Cursor
 *
C/exec sql
C+     DECLARE C1 CURSOR FOR P1
C/end-exec
 *
 *  Open cursor
 *
C/exec sql
C+     OPEN C1
C/end-exec
 *
 *  Read through file until EOF
 *
C    SQLCOD        DOUEQ     100
C/exec sql
C+     FETCH C1 USING DESCRIPTOR :SQLDA
C/end-exec
C    SQLCOD        IFNE      100
 *
 *  Extract data into print lines
 *
C                  MOVE      *BLANKS      PRTLN1
C                  MOVE      *BLANKS      PRTLN2
C                  EVAL      LINLEN = 0
C                  EVAL      POTLEN = 0
 *
C    1             DO        12            IX
C    ARR(IX)       IFNE      *BLANKS
C                  EVAL      SQLVAR = SQL_VAR(IX)
 *   Determine if exceed first print line
C    SQLTYPE       IFEQ      484
C    SQLTYPE       OREQ      488
 *     Numeric value....must extract digit length.
C                  EVAL      #DIG = (SQLLEN/256)
```

```
C                       EVAL      POTLEN = LINLEN + #DIG
C                       ELSE
 *         Character value
C                       EVAL      POTLEN = LINLEN + SQLLEN
C                       ENDIF
 *      Move data to work area.
C                       SELECT
C         ARR(IX)       WHENEQ    'CATLG#'
C                       MOVEL(P)  CATLG#        WORK
C         ARR(IX)       WHENEQ    'CATDSC'
C                       MOVEL(P)  CATDSC        WORK
C         ARR(IX)       WHENEQ    'CATDTE'
C                       MOVEL(P)  CATDTE        WORK
C         ARR(IX)       WHENEQ    'CTGRY#'
C                       MOVEL(P)  CTGRY#        WORK
C         ARR(IX)       WHENEQ    'CURYR$'
C                       MOVEL(P)  CURYR$        WORK
C         ARR(IX)       WHENEQ    'YR1$'
C                       MOVEL(P)  YR1$          WORK
C         ARR(IX)       WHENEQ    'YR2$'
C                       MOVEL(P)  YR2$          WORK
C         ARR(IX)       WHENEQ    'ONHAND'
C                       MOVEL(P)  ONHAND        WORK
C         ARR(IX)       WHENEQ    'CPRICE'
C                       MOVEL(P)  CPRICE        WORK
C         ARR(IX)       WHENEQ    'FPRICE'
C                       MOVEL(P)  FPRICE        WORK
C         ARR(IX)       WHENEQ    'PRCDTE'
C                       MOVEL(P)  PRCDTE        WORK
C         ARR(IX)       WHENEQ    'SUB#'
C                       MOVEL(P)  SUB#          WORK
C                       ENDSL
 *      Load print field
C         POTLEN        IFGT      132
C         PRTLN2        CAT       WORK:2        PRTLN2
C                       ELSE
C         PRTLN1        CAT       WORK:2        PRTLN1
C                       ENDIF
 *      Set print length.
C         SQLTYPE       IFEQ      484
C         SQLTYPE       OREQ      488
C                       EVAL      LINLEN = LINLEN + #DIG + 2
C                       ELSE
C                       EVAL      LINLEN = LINLEN + SQLLEN + 2
C                       ENDIF
C                       ENDIF
C                       ENDDO
 *    Print line(s)
C                       EXCEPT    LINE1
C         PRTLN2        IFNE      *BLANKS
C                       EXCEPT    LINE2
C                       ENDIF
 *
C                       ENDIF
 *
C                       ENDDO
 *
```

```
 *   Close the cursor
 *
C/exec sql
C+        CLOSE C1
C/end-exec
C                       MOVE      *ON          *INLR
OQPRINT    E            LINE1         1
O                       PRTLN1                 132
OQPRINT    E            LINE2         1
O                       PRTLN2                 13
```

Chapter 11

Embedded SQL Statements

This chapter contains the statements you use within an HLL program. The statements we have included are those that function solely within an embedded SQL program or that have special clauses you can use only within an HLL program.

THE BEGIN DECLARE SECTION STATEMENT

The BEGIN DECLARE SECTION statement marks the beginning of an SQL declare section. If you specify this statement, you must be sure there also is an END DECLARE SECTION statement. If you specify this statement, you can use only those variables declared within the SQL declare section as host variables.

You place the BEGIN DECLARE SECTION statement in an application program wherever variable declarations can appear. You do not use this statement in RPG or REXX programs.

The syntax of this statement is

```
BEGIN DECLARE SECTION
```

THE CALL STATEMENT

The CALL statement calls a stored procedure, which is any valid AS/400 program. Optionally, you can pass parameters to the stored procedure. The syntax of the CALL statement is

```
CALL procedure
     [(parameter [, ...]) |
      USING DESCRIPTOR descriptor]
```

Within an HLL program, you can use the USING DESCRIPTOR clause to pass the parameters. The SQLDA structure defines the descriptor (see Chapter 10 and Appendix B for information about the SQLDA). The USING DESCRIPTOR clause is valid in ILE RPG, but not valid for RPG/400 because RPG/400 cannot use the SQLDA.

THE CLOSE STATEMENT

The CLOSE statement closes an open SQL cursor within an HLL program. The cursor must already have been declared and opened before it can be closed. The syntax of the CLOSE statement is

```
CLOSE cursor name
```

The DECLARE CURSOR Statement

The DECLARE CURSOR statement defines an SQL select statement to an HLL program. The actual SELECT statement is not executed until the OPEN statement opens the cursor. The syntax of the DECLARE CURSOR statement is

```
DECLARE cursor name [INSENSITIVE | [DYNAMIC] SCROLL]  CURSOR
            [WITH HOLD]  FOR  select statement
```

1. This statement defines a cursor over the CATALOG file, selecting all fields and records.

```
DECLARE C1 CURSOR FOR
 SELECT * FROM CATALOG
```

2. In this case, you must have issued a PREPARE statement before the DECLARE statement. For example,

```
PREPARE P1 FROM :S1
```

S1 is a host variable that contains the actual SELECT statement.

```
DECLARE C1 CURSOR FOR P1
```

The cursor name you specify must be unique within the HLL program. You must specify the DECLARE CURSOR statement within the source *before* the OPEN statement.

The INSENSITIVE keyword indicates that the cursor is not sensitive to any inserts, updates or deletes to the underlying database. In this case, specifying this keyword causes the cursor to be read-only, which means that the SELECT statement cannot contain the FOR UPDATE clause. With INSENSITIVE specified the AS/400 will use a temporary result set if necessary.

The SCROLL keyword indicates that the cursor is scrollable, which means that the cursor may or may not be sensitive to inserts, updates, and deletes performed by other activation groups. When you specify SCROLL, the cursor is read-only, which means the SELECT statement cannot contain the FOR UPDATE clause.

If you specify DYNAMIC SCROLL, you can update the cursor as long as the select does not cause creation of a temporary table and as long as the select statement does not include a subselect.

You use the WITH HOLD keywords to prevent the cursor from being closed during a commit operation.

You can either explicitly define the specified select statement within the DECLARE CURSOR statement or you can reference it from a statement name. You cannot change an explicitly defined select statement except when you use host variables.

You derive a select statement referenced by a statement name via the PREPARE statement, which lets you build a SELECT statement dynamically.

The DECLARE PROCEDURE Statement

The DECLARE PROCEDURE statement defines a procedure to an HLL program. You execute procedures using the CALL statement. You use the DECLARE PROCEDURE statement before any CALL statements that reference the procedure. This statement applies only to static CALL statements.

The syntax of the DECLARE PROCEDURE statement is

```
DECLARE procedure name PROCEDURE
           [([IN | OUT | INOUT] parameter data_type [,...])]
           [RESULT (SET | SETS) integer]
           [[EXTERNAL | EXTERNAL NAME] program]
           [LANGUAGE [C | C++ | CL | COBOL | COBOLLE | FORTRAN |
                    PLI | REXX | RPG | RPGLE]]
           [PARAMETER STYLE] [GENERAL | GENERAL WITH NULLS}
           [VARIANT | NOT VARIANT]
           [SPECIFIC specific name]
           [[NOT] DETERMINISTIC]
           [CONTAINS SQL | NO SQL | READS SQL DATA | MODIFIES SQL DATA]
```

The only required item in the above statement is the name of the procedure. If you don't specify any other parameters, the program name is assumed to be the same as the name of the procedure.

You can define the parameters the procedure uses immediately *after* the procedure name. You can specify a maximum of 255 parameters for a single procedure. You define each parameter as an input (IN), output (OUT), or input-output (INOUT) parameter; the default is IN. You give each parameter a name when you define the procedure. You also must specify the data type of the parameter. For a list of the valid data types, see the CREATE TABLE statement in Chapter 8.

If the name of the program is not the same as the procedure, you must specify the EXTERNAL NAME clause, which links the actual AS/400 program name to the procedure name. You can use either the EXTERNAL NAME clause or the EXTERNAL clause for the same results.

If you wish, you can specify the language used to create the AS/400 program. If you don't specify the language, the language will be derived from the AS/400 program object itself. If the language type cannot be determined, the default is the C language.

The RESULT clause is optional; you use this clause to define the maximum number of result sets that will be returned by the procedure.

The PARAMETER STYLE clause is optional in the above statement; you use this clause strictly in association with the GENERAL clause.

The GENERAL clause specifies a simple call to the program. No additional arguments are passed for indicator variables (we discussed indicator variables in Chapter 10).

GENERAL WITH NULLS specifies that an additional argument is passed when you use indicator variables.

VARIANT or NOT VARIANT is an optional clause that specifies whether the procedure will return the same result when it is called with identical input values. This clause is for information purposes only. VARIANT means the results will not be the same. NOT VARIANT means the results will always be the same. Therefore, you use VARIANT to specify that the procedure will not always return the same result when it is called with the same input values.

The SPECIFIC clause defines a name that uniquely identifies the procedure.

The DETERMINISTIC clause indicates whether the procedure will return the same results when identical input parameters are provided to the procedure on successive calls. DETERMINISTIC indicates that the same results will be provided. NOT DETERMINISTIC indicates that the same results may not result.

The CONTAINS SQL clause indicates that the procedure does include embedded SQL statements.

The NO SQL clause indicates that the procedure does not contain any embedded SQL statements.

The READS SQL DATA clause indicates that data is read in the procedure via SQL statements.

The MODIFIES SQL DATA clause indicates that data is modified in the procedure via SQL statements.

THE DECLARE STATEMENT STATEMENT

The DECLARE STATEMENT statement declares names that the PREPARE statement will reference. The syntax of the DECLARE STATEMENT statement is

```
DECLARE statement name [, ...] STATEMENT
```

The following example of the DECLARE STATEMENT,

```
DECLARE P1 STATEMENT
```

is required to issue the following PREPARE statement:

```
PREPARE P1 FROM :S1
```

THE DECLARE VARIABLE STATEMENT

The DECLARE VARIABLE statement changes the subtype of a character field or the CCSID of a field. You must define the host variable name to the program. The syntax of the DECLARE VARIABLE statement is

```
DECLARE host variable [, ...] VARIABLE [FOR SBCS DATA  |
                                        FOR MIXED DATA |
                                        FOR BIT DATA   |
                                        CCSID integer  |
                                           DATE |
                                           TIME |
                                           TIMESTAMP]
```

1. Assume you have a field called CHRDTA defined as a character field with a length of 10. The following statement changes this field to a mixed-data character field:

```
DECLARE :CHRDTA VARIABLE FOR MIXED DATA
```

FOR SBCS DATA above indicates that the values of the field contain SBCS (single-byte character set) data.

FOR MIXED DATA indicates that the values of the field contain both SBCS and DBCS (double-byte character set) data.

FOR BIT DATA indicates that the value of the field is not associated with a character set. This type of data is never converted.

CCSID indicates that the value of the field is associated with a specific coded character set on the AS/400.

DATE indicates that the value of the field contains date data.

TIME indicates that the value of the field contains time data.

TIMESTAMP indicates that the value of the field contains timestamp data.

THE DELETE STATEMENT

When you issue the DELETE statement with an HLL program, you can either use the form of the statement found in Chapter 3, or you can delete a record from an open cursor, known as a positioned delete. The syntax of the DELETE statement is

```
DELETE FROM file name [AS correlation name]
    WHERE CURRENT OF cursor name
```

1. This statement deletes the current record fetched from cursor C1.

```
DELETE FROM CATALOG WHERE CURRENT OF C1
```

With a positioned delete, you must read a record from an open cursor in the HLL program. The DELETE statement using the WHERE CURRENT OF clause indicates that only the current record read from the cursor is to be deleted. You use the FETCH statement to read the current record.

THE DESCRIBE STATEMENT

The DESCRIBE statement obtains information about a prepared statement. You must already have used the PREPARE statement to define the statement name referenced in the DESCRIBE statement. The DESCRIBE statement is valuable when you are doing variable-field selection (see Chapter 9 for information regarding variable-field selection).

The format of the DESCRIBE statement is

```
DESCRIBE statement name INTO descriptor
    [USING {NAMES | SYSTEM NAMES | LABELS |
        ANY | BOTH | ALL}]
```

1. This statement acquires the field information from a PREPARE statement called P1.

```
DESCRIBE P1 INTO :SQLDA USING NAMES
```

The descriptor identifies the SQLDA descriptor area. Before the program issues the DESCRIBE statement, you must set the SQLN variable to a value greater than or equal to 0.

The USING clause indicates what value will be placed in the SQLNAME field in the SQLDA. If you do not specify the USING clause, the default is the same as saying USING NAMES. If there is no information to retrieve about the field, SQLNAME will be set to a zero-length string.

NAMES uses the name of the field.

SYSTEM NAMES uses the AS/400 field name.

LABELS uses the label assigned to the field.

ANY uses the label assigned to the field. If no label is available, the field name is used.

BOTH uses both the label and name of the field. In this case, two occurrences of SQLVAR per field are needed to accommodate the additional information.

ALL uses the label, field name, and AS/400 field name. In this case, three occurrences of SQLVAR per field are needed to accommodate the additional information.

THE DESCRIBE TABLE STATEMENT

The DESCRIBE TABLE statement obtains information about a specific file. The host variable contains the name of a valid file. The syntax of the DESCRIBE TABLE statement is

```
DESCRIBE TABLE host variable INTO descriptor
     [USING {NAMES | SYSTEM NAMES | LABELS |
              ANY | BOTH | ALL}]
```

1. This statement acquires the field information for the file name specified in the variable called FILE.

```
DESCRIBE TABLE :FILE INTO :SQLDA USING NAMES
```

The descriptor identifies the SQLDA descriptor area. Before you issue the DESCRIBE TABLE statement, you must set the SQLN variable to a value greater than or equal to 0.

You use the USING clause to indicate the value to be placed in the SQLNAME field in the SQLDA. If you do not specify USING, the default is the same as saying USING NAMES. If there is no information to retrieve about the field, SQLNAME is set to a zero-length string.

NAMES uses the name of the field.

SYSTEM NAMES uses the AS/400 field name.

LABELS uses the label assigned to the field.

ANY uses the label assigned to the field. If no label is available, the field name is used.

BOTH uses both the label and the name of the field. In this case, two occurrences of SQLVAR per field are needed to accommodate the additional information.

ALL uses the label, field name, and AS/400 field name. In this case, three occurrences of SQLVAR per field are needed to accommodate the additional information.

THE END DECLARE SECTION STATEMENT

The END DECLARE SECTION statement marks the end of an SQL declare section. If you specify this statement, you also must specify a BEGIN DECLARE SECTION statement. You cannot use the END DECLARE SECTION statement in RPG or REXX programs. The syntax of this statement is

```
END DECLARE SECTION
```

THE EXECUTE STATEMENT

The EXECUTE statement executes a prepared SQL statement. The syntax of the EXECUTE statement is

```
EXECUTE statement name [USING host variable [, ...]  |
                         USING DESCRIPTOR descriptor
```

1. This statement executes the prepared statement P1 passing the host variables VAR1 and VAR2 to the statement.

```
EXECUTE P1 USING :VAR1, :VAR2
```

The P1 statement might contain something like this:

```
INSERT INTO FILEA (FIELD1, FIELD2) VALUES(?,?)
```

If the prepared statement contains parameter markers (see Chapter 9), you use the USING or USING DESCRIPTOR clause to set the values for the parameter markers.

You can list the host variables to pass via the USING clause. In this case, you separate each host variable with commas. You also can use the SQLDA descriptor to pass the host variable values. In this case, you must load the SQLDA with the valid descriptions of the host variables.

Because RPG/400 does not support the SQLDA, you cannot use the USING DESCRIPTOR clause. You can, however, use this clause with ILE RPG. In RPG/400, you must specify the host variables via the USING clause only.

The **EXECUTE IMMEDIATE** Statement

The EXECUTE IMMEDIATE statement executes an SQL statement without any preparation. This statement combines the function of the PREPARE and EXECUTE statements into a single operation. The syntax of the EXECUTE IMMEDIATE statement is

```
EXECUTE IMMEDIATE  {host variable | string}
```

If you execute a statement more than once, it is more efficient to use the PREPARE and EXECUTE statements instead of the EXECUTE IMMEDIATE statement.

You can either hard-code the SQL statement you want to execute in the EXECUTE IMMEDIATE statement or you can place it in a host variable. The SQL statement itself cannot contain any host variables or parameter markers.

You can execute only the following SQL statements with the EXECUTE IMMEDIATE statement:

ALTER TABLE	DROP
CALL	GRANT
COMMENT ON	INSERT
COMMIT	LABEL ON
CREATE COLLECTION	LOCK TABLE
CREATE INDEX	RENAME
CREATE PROCEDURE	REVOKE
CREATE TABLE	ROLLBACK
CREATE VIEW	SET TRANSACTION
DELETE	UPDATE

1. This statement deletes every record from the CATALOG file.

```
EXECUTE IMMEDIATE  DELETE FROM CATALOG
```

2. This statement executes the statement found in the variable called STRING.

```
EXECUTE IMMEDIATE :STRING
```

The **FETCH** Statement

The FETCH statement retrieves either a single record or many records from an open cursor. You can think of the FETCH statement as a READ statement in RPG. The syntax of the FETCH statement is

```
FETCH [[NEXT | PRIOR | FIRST | LAST | BEFORE |
          AFTER | CURRENT | RELATIVE {host variable |
                                            integer}] FROM]
        cursor {INTO host variable [, ...] |
                INTO DESCRIPTOR descriptor  |
                FOR host variable | integer ROWS
                  [INTO host structure  |
                   USING DESCRIPTOR descriptor
```

```
            INTO host identifier 1
              [[INDICATOR] host identifier 2]]}
```

1. This statement retrieves the next record from cursor C1 and places the values in variables VAR1 and VAR2.

   ```
   FETCH C1 INTO :VAR1, :VAR2
   ```

2. Assume a data structure named DS1 contains the two variables VAR1 and VAR2. In this case,

   ```
   FETCH C1 INTO :DS1
   ```

   retrieves the fields into the data structure called DS1, which in turn maps to the variables VAR1 and VAR2.

The first keyword indicates where to position the cursor before the FETCH is executed. You must have defined the cursor with SCROLL on the DECLARE CURSOR statement if you use any of these values, with the exception of NEXT.

NEXT positions the cursor to the next record, like a READ op-code does in RPG.

PRIOR positions the cursor to the preceding record, like a READP opcode does in RPG.

FIRST positions the cursor to the first record, like the *LOVAL SETLL and READ opcodes do in RPG.

LAST positions the cursor to the last record, like the *HIVAL SETGT and READP opcode do in RPG.

BEFORE positions the cursor to before the first record, like a *LOVAL SETLL opcode does in RPG.

AFTER positions the cursor to after the last record, like a *HIVAL SETGT opcode does in RPG.

CURRENT positions the cursor to the same record it currently designates, which is the same as saying, "Read the same record again." However, if the current record has been updated and the update causes the record to change position in the cursor, an error will occur.

RELATIVE positions the cursor for a given number of records either forward or backward from the current record. You can either specify a host variable that contains the number of records to move, or you can hard-code an integer value, which can be either positive or negative.

If you specify any of the positioning keywords, you must specify the keyword FROM immediately after the positioning keyword.

After you specify the positioning of the cursor, you must specify the name of the cursor from which a record or records will be retrieved. You must open the cursor.

Next you must specify where the retrieved values are to be placed. You can specify either single- or a multiple-record retrieval.

For single-record retrieval, you can either specify the host variable names that will receive the values directly via the USING clause, or you can retrieve the field values into the SQLDA via the USING DESCRIPTOR clause. In both cases, only a single record is retrieved from the open cursor.

If you specify the USING clause, list the host variable names, each separated by commas. Instead of specifying each individual host variable, you can build a data structure that maps to the fields retrieved. Then you can specify just the name of the data structure instead of every host variable.

Specifying the USING DESCRIPTOR clause references the name of the SQLDA descriptor area.

For multiple-record retrieval, you specify the FOR ROWS clause. In this clause, you must specify the number of records to retrieve. This number can either be a hard-coded integer value or it can be a host variable.

After the FOR ROWS clause, you specify either a host structure to contain the records or you can specify the SQLDA descriptor area.

If you use the INTO clause, you specify a host variable name that refers to the host structure. A host structure is a defined area that contains each record retrieved, which is a multiple-occurrence data structure for RPG programs. Each occurrence of the data structure contains a single record.

If you use the USING DESCRIPTOR clause, you specify the name of the SQLDA descriptor area. Next you must specify the INTO subclause, which contains a host variable that points to a storage allocation area that will hold all the records retrieved. The storage allocation area must be big enough to hold all the records to be retrieved.

You optionally can define an indicator area, which you place after the first host identifier. You must specify this indicator area if any field retrieved can contain a null variable.

THE GRANT (PACKAGE) STATEMENT

The GRANT package statement lets specific user profiles access a given SQL package. You can either enter this statement within an HLL program or you can run it interactively. The syntax of the GRANT package statement is

```
GRANT {ALL [PRIVILAGES] | EXECUTE | ALTER}
      ON PACKAGE package name [, ...]
      FROM [user name | PUBLIC] [, ...]
      [WITH GRANT OPTION]
```

You can grant ALL privileges, only the EXECUTE privileges, or only the ALTER privileges.

1. This statement grants USER1 all privileges to the package named PACK1.

```
GRANT ALL ON PACKAGE PACK1 FROM USER1
```

2. This statement grants the right to alter the packages named PACK1, PACK2, and PACK3 to user profiles USER1, USER2, USER3, and USER4.

```
GRANT ALTER ON PACKAGE PACK1, PACK2, PACK3
     FROM USER1, USER2, USER3, USER4
```

EXECUTE grants the rights to execute statements in the package. ALTER allows the use of the COMMENT ON and LABEL ON statements against the package.

You can specify more than one package name within the ON PACKAGE clause. However, you must specify at least one package name, and you must separate each package name with commas.

You can specify more than one user profile within the TO clause. However, you must specify at least one user profile, and you must separate each user profile with commas.

PUBLIC grants privileges for the *PUBLIC authority.

The WITH GRANT OPTION clause lets the user profiles specified in the TO clause grant privileges to yet other users. Individual users can never grant more rights than they themselves have.

THE INCLUDE STATEMENT

The INCLUDE statement inserts declarations or statements into a source program. The syntax of the INCLUDE statement is

```
INCLUDE {SQLCA | SQLDA | member name}
```

1. Here's an example of the INCLUDE statement:

```
INCLUDE SQLDA
```

SQLCA refers to the SQL communications area, the area through which you communicate to your HLL program the results of executing SQL statements (see Appendix B for the layout of this area). In RPG programs, the SQL communications area is automatically brought into the program, so you should not specify SQLCA for RPG programs.

SQLDA refers to the SQL descriptor area, where information about fields is placed. You cannot specify SQLDA for RPG/400 programs. You can, however, specify it for ILE RPG programs.

Finally, you can specify a source member name from which HLL language statements and/or SQL statements are placed into your HLL program. You specify the file that contains this member in the INCFILE parameter of the CRTSQLxxx command.

THE INSERT INTO STATEMENT

When used within an HLL program, the INSERT INTO statement lets you insert multiple rows within a single statement. You do this by building a host structure, where each element of the host structure is a single record to be inserted. In RPG, a host structure is a multiple-occurrence data structure.

The syntax of the INSERT INTO statement is

```
INSERT INTO file name [(field name [, ...])]
        {host variable | integer} ROWS VALUES (host structure)
```

1. Here is an example using the INSERT INTO clause with the ROWS clause:

```
INSERT INTO FILEA 10 ROWS VALUES (:DS1)
```

When you use this form, you specify the number of records to insert either by hard-coding the value or by specifying a host variable that contains the number of records to insert.

Next, you specify the ROWS VALUES clause. Then you specify the name of the host structure within parentheses.

THE OPEN STATEMENT

The OPEN statement opens a defined cursor. You can think of this as a database file open operation. The SELECT statement the cursor references is executed at this time, although no records are returned to your HLL program yet.

The syntax of the OPEN statement is

```
OPEN cursor   [USING host variable [, ...]  |
              USING DESCRIPTOR descriptor]
```

1. This statement opens the cursor called C1.

```
OPEN C1
```

2. This statement opens the cursor called C1, passing the variables VAR1 and VAR2 to the statement defined in the cursor.

```
OPEN C1 USING :VAR1, :VAR2
```

You must first define the name of the cursor to open using the DECLARE CURSOR statement. You must locate the DECLARE CURSOR statement *before* the OPEN statement in your source file.

When you open a cursor, if that cursor uses parameter markers, you must pass the values to the statement. You can do this either by explicitly listing the host variables with the USING clause or by reference from the SQLDA descriptor area with the USING DESCRIPTOR clause.

If you specify the USING clause, list the host variable names, each separated by commas. Instead of specifying each individual host variable, you can build a data structure that maps to the fields to be passed. Then you can specify just the name of the data structure instead of every host variable.

The USING DESCRIPTOR clause references the name of the SQLDA descriptor area.

THE PREPARE STATEMENT

The PREPARE statement creates an executable form of an SQL statement. After you prepare an SQL statement, you can execute it via the EXECUTE statement. The syntax of the PREPARE statement is

```
PREPARE statement name [INTO descriptor
                        [USING {NAMES | SYSTEM NAMES |
                                LABELS | ANY | BOTH | ALL}]
                    FROM {host variable | string}]
```

1. Here is an example of the PREPARE statement:

```
PREPARE P1 FROM :SQLSTR
```

The statement name refers to the name assigned to this particular prepared SQL statement.

You use the INTO clause to place information into the SQLDA descriptor area, which is the same as issuing a DESCRIBE statement for the prepared name.

The USING subclause indicates what value is to be placed in the SQLNAME field in the SQLDA. If you do not specify USING, the default is the same as saying USING NAMES. If there is no information to retrieve about the field, SQLNAME is set to a zero-length string.

The NAMES clause uses the name of the field.

The SYSTEM NAMES clause uses the AS/400 field name.

The LABELS clause uses the label assigned to the field.

The ANY clause uses the label assigned to the field. If no label is available, the clause uses the field name.

The BOTH clause uses both the label and the field name. In this case, two occurrences of SQLVAR per field are necessary to accommodate the additional information.

The ALL clause uses the label, field name, and AS/400 field name. In this case, three occurrences of SQLVAR per field are necessary to accommodate the additional information.

The FROM clause specifies the SQL string to be prepared. You almost always do this with a host variable, but in PL/I, you can use a string expression instead of a host variable. The statement contained in the host variable cannot reference host variables. However, you can place parameter markers within the string.

You can prepare only the following SQL statements:

ALTER TABLE	GRANT
CALL	INSERT
COMMENT ON	LABEL ON
COMMIT	LOCK TABLE
CREATE COLLECTION	RENAME
CREATE INDEX	REVOKE
CREATE TABLE	ROLLBACK

CREATE PROCEDURE   SELECT
CREATE VIEW   SET TRANSACTION
DELETE   UPDATE
DROP

THE REVOKE (PACKAGE) STATEMENT

The REVOKE package statement prevents specific user profiles from accessing a given package. You can either enter this statement within an HLL program or you can run it interactively. The syntax of the REVOKE (package) statement is

```
REVOKE {ALL [PRIVILAGES] | EXECUTE | ALTER}
       ON PACKAGE package name [, ...]
       FROM [user name | PUBLIC] [, ...]
```

1. This statement revokes all privileges for USER1 to the package named PACK1.

```
REVOKE ALL ON PACKAGE PACK1 FROM USER1
```

2. This statement revokes the right to alter the packages named PACK1, PACK2, and PACK3 for user profiles USER1, USER2, USER3, and USER4.

```
REVOKE ALTER ON PACKAGE PACK1, PACK2, PACK3
   FROM USER1, USER2, USER3, USER4
```

You can revoke ALL privileges, only the EXECUTE privileges, or only the ALTER privileges.

The EXECUTE statement revokes the rights to execute statements in the package. The ALTER statement prevents the use of the COMMENT ON and LABEL ON statements against the package.

You can specify more than one package name within the ON PACKAGE subclause. However, you must specify at least one package name, and you must separate each name with commas.

You can specify more than one user profile within the FROM subclause. However, you must specify at least one user profile and you must separate each profile with commas. The PUBLIC statement revokes the privileges for the *PUBLIC authority.

THE SELECT STATEMENT

When used in an HLL program, the SELECT statement lets you specify two additional clauses, which indicate the type of read that is to take place on the file. All the other clauses are still valid. The syntax of the SELECT statement is

```
SELECT . . .
       [FOR UPDATE [OF field [, ...]]]
       [FOR [READ | FETCH] ONLY]
```

The FOR UPDATE clause indicates which fields in the record you can change using the UPDATE statement. You cannot use this clause for a read-only select.

If you do not specify any field names, you can change every updatable field in the record. If you specify field names, you must separate them with commas. In this case, only those fields that you specify can be updated with an UPDATE statement.

When you use the FOR UPDATE clause, the record in the file is locked.

You use the FOR READ ONLY clause to indicate that this SELECT statement is to be read-only. This means that you cannot update or delete the record, and it also prevents a record lock on the file.

THE SELECT INTO STATEMENT

The SELECT INTO statement is a special version of the SELECT statement. With this version, you extract only one record from the SELECT statement. The values for that record are placed into host variables. The syntax of the SELECT INTO statement is

```
SELECT field [, ...] INTO host variable [, ...]
   FROM ...
  WHERE ...
  GROUP BY ...
 HAVING ...
  ORDER BY ...
   WITH ...
```

1. This statement returns the highest last-year sales from the catalog master file into the variable called MAXSLS.

```
SELECT MAX(YR1$) INTO :MAXSLS
   FROM CATALOG
```

2. This statement returns last-year and previous-year sales from the catalog master file for a specific catalog number.

```
SELECT YR1$,YR2$ INTO :YR1SLS,:YR2SLS
   FROM CATALOG
  WHERE CATLG# = :PART#
```

The SELECT, INTO, and FROM clauses are required; the other clauses are optional.

You specify the keyword INTO immediately after the fields being retrieved. After the INTO keyword, you specify the host variables, separated by commas. You can either specify individual host variables or you can reference a data structure that corresponds to the fields being extracted. If you use a data structure, you specify the name of the structure instead of the individual fields.

The only other clauses you can use with the INTO version are FROM, WHERE, GROUP BY, HAVING, ORDER BY, and WITH.

We should note here that the GROUP BY clause implies that more than one record will be retrieved. In this case, you more than likely will specify the HAVING clause as well.

If the result of the SELECT clause is more than one record, an error occurs and no data is passed back to your HLL program.

THE SET OPTION STATEMENT

The SET OPTION statement defines the processing options that the SQL statements will use. The syntax of the SET OPTION statement is

```
SET OPTION {COMMIT = {*CHG | *NONE | *CS | *ALL | *RR}  |
            DECMPT = {*PERIOD | *COMMA | *SYSVAL | *JOB}          |
            NAMING = {*SYS | *SQL}                                |
            DATFMT = {*JOB | *ISO | *EUR | *USA |
                      *JIS | *MDY | *DMY | *YMD |
                      *JUL}                                       |
            DATSEP = {*JOB | *SLASH | '/' | *PERIOD |
                      '.' | *COMMA | ',' | *DASH |
                      '-' | *BLANK | ' '}                         |
            TIMFMT = {*HMS | *ISO | *EUR | *USA | *JIS} |
            TIMSEP = {*JOB | *COLON | ':' | *PERIOD |
                      '.' | *COMMA | ',' | *BLANK |
                      ' '}                                        |
            SRTSEQ = {*JOB | *HEX | *JOBRUN |
                      *LANGIDUNQ | *LANGIDSHR |
                      [*LIBL | *CURLIB | library]
                      sort table name}                           |
            LANGID = {*JOB | *JOBRUN | language id [, ...] }
            ALWBLK = {*READ | *NONE | *ALLREAD}
            ALWCPYDTA = {*YES | *NO | *OPTIMIZE}
            CLOSQLCSR = {*ENDACTGRP | *ENDMOD | *ENDPGM |
                                      *ENDSQL | *ENDJOB}
            CNULRQD = {*YES | *NO}
            DFTRDBCOL = {*NONE | library name}
            DLYPRP = {*YES | *NO}
            DYNUSRPRF = {*OWNER | *USER}
            RDBCNNMTH = {*DUW | *RUW}
            USRPRF = {*OWNER | *USER | *NAMING}
```

1. This statement sets the job to have a commit level of read stability, to use the SQL naming standards, and to use the *ISO format for date fields.

   ```
   SET OPTION  COMMIT=*ALL, NAMING=SQL, DATFMT=*ISO
   ```

   COMMIT specifies the isolation level to be used.
   *CHG specifies an isolation level of uncommitted read (UR).
   *NONE specifies an isolation level of no commit (NC).
   *CS specifies an isolation level of cursor stability (CS).
   *ALL specifies an isolation level of read stability (RS).
   *RR specifies an isolation level of repeatable read (RR).
   DECMPT specifies the symbol that will be used to represent a decimal point.
   *PERIOD uses a period as the decimal point.
   *COMMA uses a comma as the decimal point.

*SYSVAL uses the system value QDECFMT as the decimal point.

NAMING specifies whether SQL or AS/400 naming standards will be used.

*SYS indicates that AS/400 naming standards will be used.

*SQL indicates that SQL naming standards will be used.

DATFMT specifies the format of date fields.

*JOB indicates that the default for the currently running job will be used.

*ISO (International Standards Organization) indicates that a date format of *yyyy-mm-dd* will be used.

*EUR (European) indicates that a date format of *dd.mm.yyyy* will be used.

*USA (United States) indicates that a date format of *mm/dd/yyyy* will be used.

*JIS (Japanese Industrial Standard) indicates that a date format of *yyyy-mm-dd* will be used.

*MDY (Month/Day/Year) indicates that a date format of *mm/dd/yy* will be used.

*YMD (Year/Month/Day) indicates that a date format of *yy/mm/dd* will be used.

*JUL (Julian) indicates that a date format of *yy/ddd* will be used.

DATSEP specifies the character to be used as the date separator for date fields.

*JOB indicates that the default for the currently running job is used.

*SLASH or '/' indicates that a slash (/) is used.

*PERIOD or '.' indicates that a period (.) is used.

*COMMA or ',' indicates that a comma (,) is used.

*DASH or '-' indicates that a dash (-) is used.

*BLANK or 's' indicates that a blank ( ) is used.

TIMFMT specifies the format of time fields.

*HMS (Hours/Minutes/Seconds) indicates that a time format of *hh.mm.ss* will be used.

*ISO (International Standards Organization) indicates that a time format of *hh.mm.ss* will be used.

*EUR (European) indicates that a time format of *hh.mm.ss* will be used.

*USA (United States) indicates that a time format of *hh:mm* AM or *hh:mm* PM will be used.

*JIS (Japanese Industrial Standard) indicates that a time format of *hh:mm:ss* will be used.

TIMSEP specifies the character to be used as the time separator for time fields.

*JOB indicates that the default separator will be used for the currently running job.

*COLON or ':' indicates that a colon (:) will be used.

*PERIOD or '.' indicates that a period (.) will be used.

*COMMA or ',' indicates that a comma (,) will be used.

*BLANK or ' ' indicates that a blank ( ) will be used.

SRTSEQ specifies the sort sequence to be used for string comparisons.

*JOB or *JOBRUN specifies that you use the default sort sequence for the currently running job.

*HEX indicates that you do not use a sort table. The hexadecimal values of the characters determine the sort.

*LANGIDUNQ indicates that the sort sequence must contain a unique weight for each character in the code page as indicated by the LANGID value.

*LANGIDSHR indicates that the sort sequence is a shared-weight sort table for the LANGID specified.

Sort table name is the actual name of a table on the AS/400 that is used for this program. You optionally can specify the library name, or *LIBL (library list), or *CURLIB (current library).

LANGID specifies the language identifier to be used with either SRTSEQ(*LANGIDUNQ) or SRTSEQ(*LANGIDSHR).

*JOB or *JOBRUN indicates to use the default for the currently running job.

Language id indicates that a specific language identifier will be used.

ALWBLK specifies whether record blocking is allowed for read-only processing.

*READ specifies that records are blocked for read-only processing when there is no commitment control being used.

*NONE specifies that records are not blocked.

*ALLREAD specifies that record blocking can be used when commitment control is being used.

ALWCPYDTA specifies whether the system can use a temporary hold area for records when processing the SQL request.

*YES specifies that a copy of the data is allowed. This will cause the cursor to become read-only.

*NO specifies that a copy of the data is not allowed.

*OPTIMIZE specifies that the system will decide whether to get the data directly from the database or from a copy of the data.

CLOSQLCSR specifies when SQL cursors are implicitly closed.

*ENDACTGRP specifies that SQL cursors are to be closed when the current activation group ends.

*ENDMOD specifies that SQL cursors are to be closed when the module is exited.

*ENDPGM specifies that SQL cursors are to be closed when the current program ends.

*ENDSQL specifies that SQL cursors are to be closed when the highest level program in the stack that contains an SQL OPEN is ended.

*ENDJOB specifies that SQL cursors are to be closed when the job ends.

CNULRQD specifies whether a NULL-terminator is returned for character and graphic strings in C or C++ languages.

*YES specifies that a NULL-terminator is returned.

*NO specifies that a NULL-terminator is not returned.

DFTRDBCOL specifies the collection or library name to use when tables, aliases, views, indexes are not qualified in SQL statements.

*NONE specifies that no collection or library name is to be used. This means that the *LIBL will be searched for the object.

Library name specifies the name of the library to use.

DLYPRP specifies whether the validation of prepared SQL statements (PREPARE statement) are delayed until the issue of an OPEN, EXECUTE or DESCRIBE statement. Delaying validation can improve performance by eliminating redundant validations.

*YES specifies that prepared statements are to be delayed.

*NO specifies that prepared statements are not to be delayed.

DYNUSRPRF specifies the user profile to be used for dynamic SQL statements.

*OWNER specifies that the user profile associated with the owner of program is to be used.

*USER specifies that the user profile associated with the user running the program is to be used.

RDBCNNMTH specifies the semantics to be used when using the CONNECT statement.

*DUW specifies that the connection is to be made to support distributive units of work (*DUW).

*RUW specifies that the connection is to be made to support remote units of work (*RUW).

USRPRF specifies the user profile to use when the program is executed.

*OWNER specifies that the user profile associated with the owner of the program is to be used.

*USER specifies that the user profile associated with the job executing the program is to be used.

*NAMING specifies that the user profile is determined by the naming construct for the program. If *SYS is specified, *USER will be used. If *SQL is specified, *OWNER will be used.

THE SET RESULT SETS STATEMENT

The SET RESULT SETS statement identifies one or more result sets to be returned from a procedure called via an ODBC client. The syntax of the SET RESULT SETS statement is

```
SET RESULT SETS {ARRAY host structure FOR host variable ROWS  |
                CURSOR cursor |
                NONE  [, ...] }
```

The following is an example of the SET RESULT SETS statement:

```
SET RESULT SETS  CURSOR  C1
```

You can define up to 20 result sets for a procedure. However, an individual SET RESULT SETS statement can refer to only a single host structure.

The ARRAY clause identifies a host structure to contain the results returned to the client. In RPG, a host structure is a multiple-occurrence data structure, with each occurrence being a single record.

The FOR subclause indicates a host variable that specifies the number of records contained in the host structure. The host variable must be a numeric field and must have a value between 1 and 32,767.

The CURSOR clause identifies a specific cursor to be returned to the client. The cursor must be in an opened state (see the DECLARE CURSOR and OPEN statements in this chapter).

NONE indicates that no result sets are returned to the client.

THE UPDATE STATEMENT

When you issue the UPDATE statement with an HLL program, you can either use the form of the UPDATE statement we presented in Chapter 3 or you can update a record from an open cursor (known as a positioned update). The syntax of the UPDATE statement is

```
UPDATE file name [[AS] correlation name]
   SET [field = (value | NULL | DEFAULT | sub-select) |
            ROW = sub-select] [, ...]
  WHERE CURRENT OF cursor
```

1. This statement adds the value of amount to the field called YR1$ for the current record fetched from cursor C1.

```
UPDATE CATALOG
   SET YR1$=YR1$ + :AMOUNT
  WHERE CURRENT OF C1
```

With a positioned update, you must read a record from an open cursor in the HLL program. The UPDATE statement using the WHERE CURRENT OF clause indicates that only the current record read from the cursor will be updated. You read the current record using the FETCH statement.

If the SELECT statement contains the FOR UPDATE clause, you can update only those fields referenced on that clause via this UPDATE statement.

THE WHENEVER STATEMENT

The WHENEVER statement specifies what action is to take place when you encounter an exception condition during the execution of an SQL statement within a program. The syntax of the WHENEVER statement is

```
WHENEVER {NOT FOUND | SQLERROR | SQLWARNING}
        {CONTINUE | {GOTO | GO TO} [:] host label}
```

First, you define the error condition to trap; then you specify the action to take whenever that error occurs.

1. Following is an example of the WHENEVER statement:

```
WHENEVER SQLERROR   GOTO :FATAL
```

NOT FOUND indicates that no record was retrieved from a FETCH statement. Also, if any SQL statement causes the SQLCOD field in the SQL communications area to have a value of 100, the condition is considered to be "not found."

SQLERROR indicates that a serious error — an error that prevented the
SQL statement from executing — occurred with an SQL statement. This means
that the SQLCOD field in the SQL communications area has a negative value.

SQLWARNING indicates that a warning condition was generated for a SQL
statement. This means that the SQLCOD field in the SQL communications area
has a positive value other than 100.

The action to take can be either to CONTINUE executing the program or
to branch to (GOTO) a specific point in the program. For RPG, the branch
point is a TAG statement. You either can specify the name of the branch point
by itself or you can preface the name with a colon (:).

You can specify the WHENEVER statement as many times as you wish
within a program. However, only the most recently executed WHENEVER for
a specific condition is in effect at a single time. This means you can have up
to three different WHENEVER conditions active at the same time.

Appendix A

Sample Database

This appendix contains a fictitious database for a mail-order company, which we created for your use with this book. The examples we have used throughout the book come from this database. Please note that we have not included every field required in a full database here. Also, we have deliberately incorporated some "bad" design into the files to show you how using SQL can help you overcome such design problems.

Our purpose is not to expound any particular design methodology with these examples; the files and the data they contain are totally fictitious.

CATEGORY

Master File

Field Name	Description	Size
CTGRY#	Category Number	3.0 P
CTDESC	Description	25 A

Data

CTGRY#	CTDESC
15	Sporting Goods
24	Home Electronics
38	Jewelry
64	Women's Apparel
156	Furniture & Accessories
348	Auto Supplies

CATALOG

Master File

Field Name	Description	Size
CATLG#	Catalog Number	20 A
CATDSC	Description	40 A
CATDTE	Date entered catalog (MDY)	6.0 S
CTGRY#	Category Number	3.0 P
CURYR$	Sales for Current Year	7.2 P

YR1$	Sales for 1 year ago	7.2 P
YR2$	Sales for 2 years ago	7.2 P
ONHAND	Quantity on hand	7.0 P
CPRICE	Current Price	7.2 P
FPRICE	Future Price	7.2 P
PRCDTE	Date future price effective (YMD)	6.0 S
SUB#	Substitute catalog number	20 A

Data

CATLG#	CATDSC	CATDTE	CTGRY#	CURYR$
A597-3996A	Sahara Desert Mummy Sleeping Bag	031689	15	0.00
A225-8037A	Pocket Size Cassette Player	091089	24	4030.00
B115-3170A	Baroque Bead Necklace	120189	38	1056.00
B501-1218D	Solid Leotard - Blue	010190	64	3750.00
C689-1192D	Knee Pants - Green	010190	64	2400.00
D805-0271C	Vinyl Bean Bag Chair	081290	156	1550.53
C871-1139C	Corduroy Bean Bag Chair	091090	156	1655.64
A658-4077A	Two-Person Pup Tent	103090	15	1964.25
A483-7921B	Case 10W40 Motor Oil	020691	348	1039.35
B489-7920B	Case 10W30 Motor Oil	020691	348	1279.20
B156-3780A	Arctic Circle Mummy Sleeping Bag	050191	15	2999.70
D362-7997A	Portable CD Player	041592	24	270.00

YR1$	YR2$	ONHAND	CPRICE	FPRICE	PRCDTE	SUB#
115.98	2799.50	0	59.99	0.00	000000	B156-3780A
26000.00	11907.00	1500	65.00	0.00	000000	
1869.00	1580.00	147	22.00	0.00	000000	
5970.00	5005.00	150	15.00	0.00	000000	
7808.00	2600.00	189	16.00	0.00	000000	
1769.41	223.92	14	32.99	34.99	921101	
3464.23	449.90	15	45.99	0.00	000000	
11523.60	629.75	100	130.95	0.00	000000	
2590.00	0.00	35	15.99	0.00	000000	B489-7920B
3237.50	0.00	30	15.99	0.00	000000	
4413.70	0.00	59	99.99	102.99	921201	
0.00	0.00	250	135.00	0.00	000000	

CUSTMAST

Master File

Field Name	Description	Size
CUST#	Customer Number	5.0 P
NAME	Customer Name	30 A
ADDR	Address	30 A
CITY	City	25 A
STATE	State	10 A
ZIP	Zip Code	10 A
CREDIT	Credit Limit	7.2 P
ONORD$	Amount on Order	7.2 P
CURYR$	Sales for Current Year	7.2 P
YR1$	Sales for 1 year ago	7.2 P
YR2$	Sales for 2 years ago	7.2 P

Data

CUST#	NAME	ADDR	CITY	STATE
392	Jane's Gift Emporium	123 Market St.	New York	NY
411	Bob & Carol's Hallway Gifts	4551 1st Ave.	Cleveland	OH
1583	Paul's Auto Store	14785 Detroit Ave.	Toronto	ONTARIO
8395	Alice's Sundries	32 East Lane	Milwaukee	WI
32418	Hemingway Travel Club	874 West Circle	Mansfield	OH
62990	Bar & Grill Health Club	129 Ridge Road	Birmingham	AL

ZIP	CREDIT	ONORD$	CURYR$	YR1$	YR2$
11205	2000.00	29.99	3266.93	21269.41	2253.82
44121-1106	500.00	220.00	4365.44	14377.93	11907.00
L8N 3K1	3600.00	1039.35	2318.55	5827.50	0.00
60158	1500.00	1319.60	929.80	1869.00	1300.00
44687	15000.00	2999.70	4963.95	11639.58	3429.25
53186	5000.00	750.00	6150.00	13778.00	6305.00

ORDERHDR

Master File

Field Name	Description	Size
STATUS	Order Header Status	1 A
ORDER#	Order Number	5.0 P
CUST#	Customer Number	5.0 P
ENTDTE	Date Order Entered (YMD)	6.0 S

Data

STATUS	ORDER#	CUST#	ENTDTE
C	1034	32418	891215
C	1069	62990	900315
C	1108	411	900510
C	1187	392	900606
C	1212	8395	900815
C	1226	392	900815
C	1227	62990	901205
C	1228	32418	901205
C	1246	32418	910227
C	1259	411	910228
C	1272	1583	910504
C	1273	62990	910616
O	1314	392	910619
C	1316	392	910729
C	1328	392	910911
C	1360	32418	911006
C	1362	1583	911008
C	1365	8395	911010
O	1375	411	911115
C	1400	411	920114
C	1401	62990	920114
O	1410	8395	920301
O	1411	411	920301
C	1420	392	920315
O	1423	32418	920315
O	1469	1583	920420
C	1470	32418	920420
C	1483	411	920425
O	1492	62990	920426

ORDERITM

Master File

Field Name	Description	Size
STATUS	Order Item Status	1 A
ORDER#	Order Number	5.0 P
CATLG#	Catalog Number	20 A
ORDQTY	Order Quantity	7.0 P
SHPQTY	Quantity Shipped	7.0 P
PRICE	Unit Price	7.2 P

Data

STATUS	ORDER#	CATLG#	ORDQTY	SHPQTY	PRICE
C	1034	A597-3996A	50	50	55.99
C	1069	C689-1192D	100	100	13.00
C	1069	B501-1218D	380	385	13.00
C	1108	A225-8037A	189	189	63.00
C	1187	B115-3170A	79	79	20.00
C	1212	C689-1192D	100	100	13.00
C	1226	D805-0271C	8	8	27.99
C	1226	C871-1139C	10	10	44.99
C	1227	B501-1218D	300	300	15.00
C	1228	A658-4077A	5	5	125.95
C	1246	A658-4077A	88	88	130.95
C	1259	C871-1139C	80	77	44.99
C	1259	A225-8037A	100	100	65.00
C	1259	B156-3780A	50	46	95.95
C	1272	B489-7920B	250	250	12.95
C	1273	B501-1218D	100	98	15.00
C	1273	C689-1192D	488	488	16.00
O	1314	D805-0271C	60	59	29.99
C	1316	B115-3170A	8	8	22.00
C	1328	A225-8037A	300	300	65.00
C	1360	A597-3996A	2	2	57.99
C	1362	A483-7921B	200	200	12.95
C	1362	B489-7920B	80	80	15.99
C	1365	B115-3170A	89	89	21.00
O	1375	B115-3170A	50	40	22.00

continued

STATUS	ORDER#	CATLG#	ORDQTY	SHPQTY	PRICE
C	1375	D805-0271C	20	20	32.99
C	1400	A225-8037A	18	18	65.00
C	1401	C689-1192D	150	150	16.00
O	1410	D805-0271C	60	20	32.99
C	1410	D362-7997A	2	2	135.00
C	1420	A225-8037A	44	44	65.00
C	1420	D805-0271C	7	7	32.99
O	1423	B156-3780A	60	30	99.99
C	1423	A658-4077A	7	7	130.95
O	1469	A483-7921B	130	65	15.99
C	1470	A658-4077A	8	8	130.95
C	1483	C871-1139C	36	36	45.99
O	1492	B501-1218D	300	250	15.00

SALESHST

Master File

Field Name	Description	Size
INV#	Invoice Number	7.0 P
ORDER#	Order Number	5.0 P
CUST#	Customer Number	5.0 P
CATLG#	Catalog Number	20 A
SHPDTE	Date Shipped (YMD)	6.0 S
SHPQTY	Quantity Shipped	7.0 P
PRICE	Price at time shipped	7.2 P
AMOUNT	Extended Amount	7.2 P

Data

INV#	ORDER#	CUST#	CATLG#	SHPDTE	SHPQTY	PRICE	AMOUNT
900251	1034	32418	A597-3996A	900125	50	55.99	2799.50
900851	1069	62990	C689-1192D	900326	100	13.00	1300.00
901021	1069	62990	B501-1218D	900412	200	13.00	2600.00
901321	1108	411	A225-8037A	900512	189	63.00	11907.00
901521	1069	62990	B501-1218D	900601	185	13.00	2405.00
901671	1187	392	B115-3170A	900616	79	20.00	1580.00
902531	1212	8395	C689-1192D	900910	50	13.00	650.00

continued

INV#	ORDER#	CUST#	CATLG#	SHPDTE	SHPQTY	PRICE	AMOUNT
903031	1212	8395	C689-1192D	901030	50	13.00	650.00
903032	1226	392	D805-0271C	901030	8	27.99	223.92
903161	1226	392	C871-1139C	901112	10	44.99	449.90
903461	1228	32418	A658-4077A	901212	5	125.95	629.75
910091	1227	62990	B501-1218D	910109	300	15.00	4500.00
910751	1246	32418	A658-4077A	910316	88	13.95	11523.60
910911	1259	411	C871-1139C	910401	77	44.99	3464.23
911311	1272	1583	B489-7920B	910511	250	12.95	3237.50
911711	1259	411	A225-8037A	910620	100	65.00	6500.00
911741	1273	62990	B501-1218D	910623	98	15.00	1470.00
911911	1273	62990	C689-1192D	910710	100	16.00	1600.00
911931	1259	411	B156-3780A	910712	46	95.95	4413.70
912521	1273	62990	C689-1192D	910909	200	16.00	3200.00
912591	1328	392	A225-8037A	910916	300	65.00	19500.00
912881	1360	32418	A597-3996A	911015	2	57.99	115.98
913011	1273	62990	C689-1192D	911028	188	16.00	3008.00
913341	1314	392	D805-0271C	911130	59	29.99	1769.41
913481	1365	8395	B115-3170A	911214	89	21.00	1869.00
913482	1362	1583	A483-7921B	911214	200	12.95	2590.00
920051	1316	392	B115-3170A	920105	8	22.00	176.00
920131	1362	1583	B489-7920B	920113	80	15.99	1279.20
920312	1375	411	B115-3170A	920131	40	22.00	880.00
920421	1401	62990	C689-1192D	920211	150	16.00	2400.00
920491	1400	411	A225-8037A	920218	18	65.00	1170.00
920601	1375	411	D805-0271C	920229	20	32.99	659.80
920701	1410	8395	D805-0271C	920310	20	32.99	659.80
920791	1423	32418	B156-3780A	920319	30	99.99	2999.70
920861	1420	392	A225-8037A	920326	10	65.00	650.00
920921	1423	32418	A658-4077A	920401	7	130.95	916.65
921091	1420	392	D805-0271C	920418	7	32.99	230.93
921221	1470	32418	A658-4077A	920501	8	130.95	1047.60
921351	1420	392	A225-8037A	920514	34	65.00	2210.00
921352	1492	62990	B501-1218D	920514	250	15.00	3750.00
921353	1483	411	C871-1139C	920514	36	45.99	1655.64
921354	1469	1583	A483-7921B	920514	35	15.99	559.65
921361	1410	8395	D362-7997A	920515	2	135.00	270.00
921421	1469	1583	A483-7921B	920521	30	15.99	479.70

Appendix B

The SQL Communications Area

When you work with SQL within an HLL program, you must have information about whether a statement has executed correctly. The SQL communications area provides this information. You use the SQL descriptor area when you work with variable field selection. This appendix shows what each of these areas contains for an RPG program.

The INCLUDE SQLCA statement brings the SQL communications area into an ILE RPG program. For RPG/400, this area is brought in automatically.

ILE RPG

```
D*        SQL Communications area
D SQLCA            DS
D  SQLAID               1      8A
D  SQLABC               9     12B 0
D  SQLCOD              13     16B 0
D  SQLERL              17     18B 0
D  SQLERM              19     88A
D  SQLERP              89     96A
D  SQLERRD             97    120B 0 DIM(6)
D  SQLERR              97    120A
D   SQLER1             97    100B 0
D   SQLER2            101    104B 0
D   SQLER3            105    108B 0
D   SQLER4            109    112B 0
D   SQLER5            113    116B 0
D   SQLER6            117    120B 0
D  SQLWRN             121    131A
D   SQLWN0            121    121A
D   SQLWN1            122    122A
D   SQLWN2            123    123A
D   SQLWN3            124    124A
D   SQLWN4            125    125A
D   SQLWN5            126    126A
D   SQLWN6            127    127A
D   SQLWN7            128    128A
D   SQLWN8            129    129A
D   SQLWN9            130    130A
D   SQLWNA            131    131A
D  SQLSTT             132    136A
D*  End of SQLCA
```

RPG/400

```
ISQLCA          DS
I                            1   8 SQLAID        SQL
I                        B   9  12ØSQLABC        SQL
I                        B  13  16ØSQLCOD        SQL
I                        B  17  18ØSQLERL        SQL
I                           19  88 SQLERM        SQL
I                           89  96 SQLERP        SQL
I                           97 12Ø SQLERR        SQL
I                        B  97 1ØØØSQLER1        SQL
I                        B 1Ø1 1Ø4ØSQLER2        SQL
I                        B 1Ø5 1Ø8ØSQLER3        SQL
I                        B 1Ø9 112ØSQLER4        SQL
I                        B 113 116ØSQLER5        SQL
I                        B 117 12ØØSQLER6        SQL
I                          121 131 SQLWRN        SQL
I                          121 121 SQLWNØ        SQL
I                          122 122 SQLWN1        SQL
I                          123 123 SQLWN2        SQL
I                          124 124 SQLWN3        SQL
I                          125 125 SQLWN4        SQL
I                          126 126 SQLWN5        SQL
I                          127 127 SQLWN6        SQL
I                          128 128 SQLWN7        SQL
I                          129 129 SQLWN8        SQL
I                          13Ø 13Ø SQLWN9        SQL
I                          131 131 SQLWNA        SQL
I                          132 136 SQLSTT        SQL
```

Table B.1 explains each field and its usage.

TABLE B.1
SQL Communications Area Fields

Field Name	Type	Description
SQLAID	CHAR(8)	Contains static text "SQLCA".
SQLABC	INTEGER	Contains the length of the SQLCA, 136.
SQLCOD	INTEGER	SQL return code. Code — Meaning 0 — Successful execution. However, warnings may have been generated. Positive — Successful execution, but with a warning condition. Negative — Error condition.
SQLERL	SMALLINT	Length for SQLERM, in the range 0 through 70. 0 means that the value of SQLERM is not pertinent.
SQLERM	CHAR(70)	Contains message replacement text associated with the SQLCODE. For CONNECT and SET CONNECTION, the SQLERM field contains information about the connection: Relational Database Name — CHAR(18) Product Identification (same as SQLERP) — CHAR(8) User ID of the server job — CHAR(10) Connection method (*DUW or *RUW) — CHAR(10)

continued

TABLE B.1 CONTINUED

Field Name	Type	Description
		DDM server class name CHAR(10)
		QAS DB2 for OS/400
		QDB2 DB2 for MVS
		QDB2/2 DB2 for OS/2
		QDB2/6000 DB2 for AIX/6000
		QDB2/HPUX DB2 for HP-UX
		QDB2/NT DB2 for NT
		QDB2/SUN DB2 for SUN
		QSQLDS/VM SQL/DS VM
		QSQLDS/VSE SQL/DS VSE
		Connection type SMALLINT
		(same as SQLER4)
SQLERP	CHAR(8)	Contains the name of the product and module returning the error. The first three characters identify the product.
		ARI for SQL/DS
		DSN for DB2 for MVS
		QSQ for DB2 for OS/400
		SQL for all other DB2 products
SQLER1	BIN(4)	Contains the last four characters of the CPF escape message if SQLCOD is less than 0. For example, if the message is CPF5715, X"F5F7F1F5" is placed in SQLER1.
SQLER2	BIN(4)	Contains the last four characters of a CPD diagnostic message if the SQL code is less than 0.
SQLER3	BIN(4)	For INSERT, UPDATE, and DELETE, shows the number of rows affected.
		For a FETCH statement, contains the number of rows fetched.
		For a CONNECT for status statement, contains information on the connection status.
		For the PREPARE statement, contains the estimated number of rows selected.
SQLER4	BIN(4)	For the PREPARE statement, contains a relative number estimate of the resources required for every execution. This number varies depending on the current availability of indexes, file sizes, CPU model, etc. It is an estimated cost for the access plan chosen by the DB2 for OS/400 Query Optimizer.
		For a CONNECT and SET CONNECTION statement, contains the type of conversation used and whether or not committable updates can be performed.
		For a FETCH statement, contains the length of the row retrieved.
SQLER5	BIN(4)	For a DELETE statement, shows the number of rows affected by referential constraints.
		For an EXECUTE IMMEDIATE or PREPARE statement, may contain the position of a syntax error. On a multiple-row FETCH statement, SQLERRD(5) contains +100 if the last row currently in the table has been fetched.
		For a CONNECT or SET CONNECTION statement, contains:
		-1 if the connection is unconnected
		0 if the connection is local
		1 if the connection is remote
SQLER6	BIN(4)	Contains the SQL completion message identifier when the SQLCOD is 0.
SQLWRN	CHAR(11)	A set of 11 warning indicators, each containing blank or W or N.
SQLWN0	CHAR(1)	Blank if all other indicators are blank; contains W if at least one other indicator contains W or N.

continued

		TABLE **B.1** CONTINUED
Field Name	Type	Description
SQLWN1	CHAR(1)	Contains W if the value of a string column was truncated when assigned to a host variable. Can contain a value of N if *NOCNULRQD was specified on the CRTSQLCI command and if the value of a string column was assigned to a C NUL-terminated host variable and if the host variable was large enough to contain the result but not large enough to contain the NUL-terminator.
SQLWN2	CHAR(1)	Contains W if the null values were eliminated from the argument of a function.
SQLWN3	CHAR(1)	Contains W if the number of columns is larger than the number of host variables.
SQLWN4	CHAR(1)	Contains W if a prepared UPDATE or DELETE statement does not include a WHERE clause.
SQLWN5	CHAR(1)	Reserved.
SQLWN6	CHAR(1)	Contains W if date arithmetic results in an end-of-month adjustment.
SQLWN7	CHAR(1)	Reserved.
SQLWN8	CHAR(1)	Contains W if the result of a character conversion contains the substitution character.
SQLWN9	CHAR(1)	Reserved.
SQLWNA	CHAR(1)	Reserved.
SQLSTT	CHAR(5)	A return code that indicates the outcome of the most recently executed SQL statement.

SQL DESCRIPTOR AREA

The SQL Descriptor is used only with ILE RPG. It is not allowed with RPG/400. The descriptor area is brought into your HLL program by means of the INCLUDE SQLDA statement.

```
D*      SQL Descriptor area
D SQLDA           DS
D   SQLDAID               1      8A
D   SQLDABC               9     12B Ø
D   SQLN                 13     14B Ø
D   SQLD                 15     16B Ø
D   SQL_VAR                     8ØA      DIM(SQL_NUM)
D                        17     18B Ø
D                        19     2ØB Ø
D                        21     32A
D                        33     48*
D                        49     64*
D                        65     66B Ø
D                        67     96A
D*
D SQLVAR          DS
D   SQLTYPE               1      2B Ø
D   SQLLEN                3      4B Ø
D   SQLRES                5     16A
D   SQLDATA              17     32*
D   SQLIND               33     48*
D   SQLNAMELEN           49     5ØB Ø
D   SQLNAME              51     8ØA
D*  End of SQLDA
```

Table B.2 explains each field and its usage.

TABLE B.2

SQL Descriptor Area Fields

Field Name	Type	Description
SQLDAID	CHAR(8)	An "eye catcher" for storage dumps, containing "SQLDA ".
SQLDABC	INTEGER	Number of bytes of storage allocated for the SQLDA.
SQLN	SMALLINT	Total number of occurrences of SQLVAR provided in the SQLDA.
SQLD	SMALLINT	Number of host variables described by SQLVAR to be used in the SQLDA when executing this statement.
SQLTYPE	SMALLINT	Indicates the data type of the host variable and whether an indicator variable is provided. 384/385 Fixed-length character-string representation of a date. 388/389 Fixed-length character-string representation of a time. 392/393 Fixed-length character-string representation of a time stamp. 400/401 NUL-terminated graphic string. 448/449 Varying-length character string. 452/453 Fixed-length character string. 456/457 Long varying-length character string. 460/461 NUL-terminated character string. 464/465 Varying-length graphic string. 468/469 Fixed-length graphic string. 472/473 Long graphic string. 476/477 PASCAL L-string. 480/481 Floating point. 484/485 Packed decimal. 488/489 Zoned decimal. 496/497 Large integer (4 bytes). 500/501 Small integer (2 bytes). 504/505 DISPLAY SIGN LEADING SEPARATE.

SQLLEN	SMALLINT	The length attribute of the host variable. If SQLTYPE has the following values, SQLLEN will contain specific information.
		480/481 Floating point.
		    4 for single
		    8 for double precision
		484/485 Packed decimal.
		    Precision in byte 1
		    Scale in byte 2
		488/489 Zoned decimal.
		    Precision in byte 1
		    Scale in byte 2
		504/505 DISPLAY SIGN LEADING SEPARATE.
		    Precision in byte 1
		    Scale in byte 2

SQLRES	CHAR(12)	Reserved.
SQLDATA	pointer	Contains the address of the host variable.
SQLIND	pointer	Contains the address of the indicator variable.
SQLNAME	VARCHAR	Contains the CCSID of the host variable.

Appendix C

SQL Performance

Finding optimum SQL performance always means finding a balance between what you want to accomplish and the effect SQL statements have on your AS/400's performance.

When you issue a query against a file or files, SQL considers many factors in its attempt to find the best method for extracting the data. When you execute a query over a single file, SQL performs very well — even over a large file. However, joining files together or using subselects can adversely affect performance.

At times it seems as if SQL has a mind of its own and that it is not predictable. You can, however, attempt to improve the performance of a SQL query with some basic procedures, which we discuss here.

INDEXES

Indexes are very useful when you create them properly. For example, if you frequently reference a field within a WHERE, GROUP BY, or HAVING clause by means of a selection predicate (=,<, or the like), an index over that field can improve performance. An index over a field also can improve performance when you use that field to join files together.

THE OPTIMIZE OPTION

When you read records from a file, you can improve performance by means of the OPTIMIZE FOR n ROWS clause in the SELECT statement. This clause instructs SQL to choose a method of record retrieval that will return the records in the quickest time possible.

THE DEBUG OPTION

When you execute SQL statements, you can use debug mode to find out exactly what SQL did in the process; by analyzing these results, you might find a better way to write the SQL statement.

To take this approach, you issue the STRDBG (Start Debug) command, then you execute your SQL statement. Next, look at the job log for your job. The job log will contain messages about exactly what occurred. By reading these messages, you will find such things as what indexes the program examined, which it used, or whether SQL created its own index. By trying the SQL statement in different ways, you can see which statement gives you the best results.

THE ALLOW COPY DATA OPTION

When you specify SQL statements, you can indicate whether SQL is allowed to copy the data to a work area. Sometimes this method enables quicker executions, especially when you are joining files together or using subselects. You can specify this method as part of the attributes for interactive query, or you can use the ALWCPYDTA parameter in an HLL program.

JOIN CONSIDERATIONS

When you join files together, especially more than two files, the more information you provide about the join the better the performance will be. For example, you might normally join FILEA to FILEB and FILEB to FILEC. However, if FILEA has the same join fields as FILEC, you specify the join condition for FILEA to FILEC in addition to specifying the FILEB-to-FILEC join.

Another thing to keep in mind is that the larger the files you are joining, the more adverse the effects on performance. Therefore, it may sometimes be in your best interest to run single SQL selects over these files, selecting the records you need and placing those records in a work file. This way, you reduce the number of records being joined together.

Index

New Books in the 29th Street Press® Library

THE AS/400 EXPERT: READY-TO-RUN RPG/400 TECHNIQUES

By Julian Monypenny and Roger Pence

As the first book in The AS/400 Expert series, *Ready-to-Run RPG/400 Techniques* provides a variety of RPG templates, subroutines, and copy modules, sprinkled with evangelical advice, to help you write robust and effective RPG/400 programs. Highlights include string-handling routines, numeric editing routines, date routines, error-handling modules, and tips for using OS/400 APIs with RPG/400. The tested and ready-to-run code building blocks — provided on an accompanying CD — easily snap into existing RPG code and integrate well with new RPG/400 projects. 203 pages.

CREATING CL COMMANDS BY EXAMPLE

By Lynn Nelson

Learn from an expert how to create CL commands that have the same functionality and power as the IBM commands you use every day. You'll see how to create commands with all the function found in IBM's commands, including parameter editing, function keys, F4 prompt for values, expanding lists of values, and conditional prompting. Whether you're in operations or programming, *Creating CL Commands by Example* can help you tap the tremendous power and flexibility of CL commands to automate tasks and enhance applications. 134 pages.

DDS KEYWORD REFERENCE

By James Coolbaugh

Reach for the *DDS Keyword Reference* when you need quick, at-your-fingertips information about DDS keywords for physical files, logical files, display files, printer files, and ICF files. In this no-nonsense volume, author Jim Coolbaugh gives you all the keywords you'll need, listed alphabetically in five sections. He explains each keyword, providing syntax rules and examples for coding the keyword. The *DDS Keyword Reference*, which is current to V4R3, is a friendly and manageable alternative to IBM's bulky DDS reference manual. 212 pages.

DDS PROGRAMMING FOR DISPLAY & PRINTER FILES, SECOND EDITION

By James Coolbaugh

DDS Programming for Display & Printer Files, Second Edition, helps you master DDS and — as a result — improve the quality of your display presentations and your printed jobs. Updated through OS/400 V4R3, the second edition offers a thorough, straightforward explanation of how to use DDS to program display files and printer files. It includes extensive DDS programming examples for CL and RPG that you can put to use immediately because a companion CD includes all the DDS, RPG, and CL source code presented in the book. 429 pages.

DOMINO AND THE AS/400: INSTALLATION AND CONFIGURATION

By Wilfried Blankertz, Rosana Choruzy, Joanne Mindzora, and Michelle Zolkos

Domino and the AS/400: Installation and Configuration gives you everything you need to implement Lotus Domino 4.6 on the AS/400, guiding you step by step through installation, configuration, customization, and administration. Here you get an introduction to Domino for AS/400 and full instructions for developing a backup and recovery plan for saving and restoring Domino data on the AS/400. 311 pages.

E-BUSINESS
Thriving in the Electronic Marketplace

By Nahid Jilovec

E-Business: Thriving in the Electronic Marketplace identifies key issues organizations face when they implement e-business projects and answers fundamental questions about entering and navigating the changing world of e-business. A concise guide to moving your business into the exciting world of collaborative e-business, the book introduces the four e-business models that drive today's economy and gives a clear summary of e-business technologies. It focuses on practical business-to-business applications. 172 pages.

ESSENTIALS OF SUBFILE PROGRAMMING
and Advanced Topics in RPG IV

By Phil Levinson

This textbook provides a solid background in AS/400 subfile programming in the newest version of the RPG language: RPG IV. Subfiles are the AS/400 tool that lets you display lists of data on the screen for user interaction. You learn to design and program subfiles, via step-by-step instructions and real-world programming exercises that build from chapter to chapter. A section on the Integrated Language Environment (ILE), introduced concurrently with RPG IV, presents tools and techniques that support effective modular programming. An instructor's kit is available. 293 pages.

IMPLEMENTING WINDOWS NT ON THE AS/400
Installing, Configuring, and Troubleshooting
By Nick Harris, Phil Ainsworth, Steve Fullerton, and Antoine Sammut
Implementing Windows NT on the AS/400: Installing, Configuring, and Troubleshooting provides everything you need to know about using NT on your AS/400, including how to install NT Server 4.0 on the Integrated Netfinity Server, synchronize user profiles and passwords between the AS/400 and NT, administer NT disk storage and service packs from the AS/400, back up NT data from the AS/400, manage NT servers on remote AS/400s, and run Windows-based personal productivity applications on the AS/400. 393 pages.

INTRODUCTION TO AS/400 SYSTEM OPERATIONS, SECOND EDITION
By Heidi Rothenbuehler and Patrice Gapen
Here's the second edition of the textbook that covers what you need to know to become a successful AS/400 system operator or administrator. Updated through V4R3 of OS/400, *Introduction to AS/400 System Operations, Second Edition*, teaches you the basics of system operations so that you can manage printed reports, perform regularly scheduled procedures, and resolve end-user problems. New material covers the Integrated File System (IFS), AS/400 InfoSeeker, Operations Navigator, and much more. 182 pages.

JAVA AND THE AS/400
Practical Examples Using VisualAge for Java
By Daniel Darnell
This detailed guide takes you through everything you need to know about the AS/400's implementation of Java, including the QShell Interpreter and the Integrated File System (IFS), and development products such as VisualAge for Java (VAJ) and the AS/400 Toolbox for Java. The author provides several small application examples that demonstrate the advantages of Java programming for the AS/400. The companion CD contains all the sample code presented in the book and full-version copies of VAJ Professional Edition and the AS/400 Toolbox for Java. 300 pages.

OPNQRYF BY EXAMPLE
By Mike Dawson and Mike Manto
The OPNQRYF (Open Query File) command is the single most dynamic and versatile command on the AS/400. Drawing from real-life, real-job experiences, the authors explain the basics and the intricacies of OPNQRYF with lots of examples to make you productive quickly. An appendix provides the UPDQRYF (Update Query File) command — a powerful addition to AS/400 and System/38 file update capabilities. 216 pages.

Also Published by 29th Street Press

CONTROL LANGUAGE PROGRAMMING FOR THE AS/400, SECOND EDITION
By Bryan Meyers and Dan Riehl, NEWS/400 technical editors
This comprehensive CL programming textbook offers students up-to-the-minute knowledge of the skills they will need in today's MIS environment. Chapters progress methodically from CL basics to more complex processes and concepts, guiding students toward a professional grasp of CL programming techniques and style. In this second edition, the authors have updated the text to include discussion of the Integrated Language Environment (ILE) and the fundamental changes ILE introduces to the AS/400's execution model. 522 pages.

DATABASE DESIGN AND PROGRAMMING FOR DB2/400
By Paul Conte
This textbook is the most complete guide to DB2/400 design and programming available anywhere. The author shows you everything you need to know about physical and logical file DDS, SQL/400, and RPG IV and COBOL/400 database programming. Clear explanations illustrated by a wealth of examples demonstrate efficient database programming and error handling with both DDS and SQL/400. 610 pages.

DEVELOPING YOUR AS/400 INTERNET STRATEGY
By Alan Arnold
This book addresses the issues unique to deploying your AS/400 on the Internet. It includes procedures for configuring AS/400 TCP/IP and information about which client and server technologies the AS/400 supports natively. This enterprise-class tutorial evaluates the AS/400 as an Internet server and teaches you how to design, program, and manage your Web home page. 248 pages.

ESSENTIALS OF SUBFILE PROGRAMMING
and Advanced Topics in RPG/400
By Phil Levinson
Essentials of Subfile Programming teaches you to design and program subfiles, offering step-by-step instructions and real-world programming exercises that build from chapter to chapter. You learn to design and create subfile records; load, clear, and display subfiles; and create pop-up windows. In addition, the advanced topics help you mine the rich store of data in the file-information and program-status data structures, handle errors, improve data integrity, and manage program-to-program communication. An instructor's manual is available. 260 pages.

IMPLEMENTING AS/400 SECURITY, THIRD EDITION
By Wayne Madden and Carol Woodbury
Concise and practical, this third edition of *Implementing AS/400 Security* not only brings together in one place the fundamental AS/400 security tools and experience-based recommendations you need but also includes specifics on the latest security enhancements available in OS/400 V4R1 and V4R2. In addition, you'll find updated chapters that cover security system values; user profiles; database security; output queue and spooled file security; using OS/400 security APIs; network security; thwarting hackers; and auditing, as well as completely new chapters that include discussions about Internet security and business contingency planning. 424 pages.

INSIDE THE AS/400, SECOND EDITION
Featuring the AS/400e series
By Frank G. Soltis
Learn from the architect of the AS/400 about the new generation of AS/400e systems and servers and about the latest system features and capabilities introduced in Version 4 of OS/400. Dr. Frank Soltis demystifies the system, shedding light on how it came to be, how it can do the things it does, and what its future may hold. 402 pages.

MASTERING THE AS/400, SECOND EDITION
A Practical, Hands-On Guide
By Jerry Fottral
With its utilitarian approach that stresses student participation, this introductory textbook to AS/400 concepts and facilities is a natural prerequisite to programming and database management courses. It emphasizes mastery of system/user interface, member-object-library relationship, use of CL commands, and basic database and program development utilities. The second edition is updated to V3R1/V3R6 and includes coverage of projection, selection, and access path with join logical files; the powerful new parameters added to the CHGPF (Change Physical File) command; and an introduction to SQL/400, with a focus on the Data Manipulation Language. Each lesson includes a lab that focuses on the essential topics presented in the lesson. 575 pages.

PROGRAMMING IN RPG IV, REVISED EDITION
By Judy Yaeger, Ph.D., a NEWS/400 *technical editor*
This textbook provides a strong foundation in the essentials of business programming, featuring the newest version of the RPG language: RPG IV. Focusing on real-world problems and down-to-earth solutions using the latest techniques and features of RPG, this book provides everything you need to know to write a well-designed RPG IV program. This revised edition includes a new section about subprocedures and an addition about using the RPG ILE source debugger. An instructor's kit is available. 435 pages.

PROGRAMMING IN RPG/400, SECOND EDITION
By Judy Yaeger, Ph.D., a NEWS/400 *technical editor*
This second edition refines and extends the comprehensive instructional material contained in the original textbook and features a new section that introduces externally described printer files, a new chapter that highlights the fundamentals of RPG IV, and a new appendix that correlates the key concepts from each chapter with their RPG IV counterparts. Includes everything you need to learn how to write a well-designed RPG program, from the most basic to the more complex. An instructor's kit is available. 481 pages.

RPG IV BY EXAMPLE

By George Farr and Shailan Topiwala

RPG IV by Example addresses the needs and concerns of RPG programmers at any level of experience. The focus is on RPG IV in a practical context that lets AS/400 professionals quickly grasp what's new without dwelling on the old. Beginning with an overview of RPG IV specifications, the authors prepare the way for examining all the features of the new version of the language. The chapters that follow explore RPG IV further with practical, easy-to-use applications. 488 pages.

RPG IV JUMP START, SECOND EDITION
Moving Ahead With the New RPG

By Bryan Meyers, a NEWS/400 *technical editor*

In this second edition of *RPG IV Jump Start*, Bryan Meyers has added coverage for new releases of the RPG IV compiler (V3R2, V3R6, and V3R7) and amplified the coverage of RPG IV's participation in the Integrated Language Environment (ILE). As in the first edition, he covers RPG IV's changed and new specifications and data types. He presents the new RPG from the perspective of a programmer who already knows the old RPG, pointing out the differences between the two language versions and demonstrating how to take advantage of the new syntax and function. 214 pages.

SUBFILE TECHNIQUE FOR RPG/400 PROGRAMMERS, SECOND EDITION

By Jonathan Yergin, CDP, and Wayne Madden

Here's the code you need for a complete library of shell subfile programs: RPG/400 code, DDS, CL, and sample data files. There's even an example for programming windows plus some "whiz bang" techniques that can add punch to your applications. The book explains the code in simple, straightforward style and tells you when each technique should be used for best results. 3.5" PC diskette included. 326 pages.

TCP/IP AND THE AS/400

By Michael Ryan

Transmission Control Protocol/Internet Protocol (TCP/IP) is fast becoming a major protocol in the AS/400 world because of TCP/IP's ubiquity and predominance in the networked world as well as its being the protocol for the Internet, intranets, and extranets. *TCP/IP and the AS/400* provides background for AS/400 professionals to understand the capabilities of TCP/IP, its strengths and weaknesses, and how to configure and administer the TCP/IP protocol stack on the AS/400. It shows TCP/IP gurus on other types of systems how to configure and manage the AS/400 TCP/IP capabilities. 362 pages.

VISUALAGE FOR RPG BY EXAMPLE

By Bryan Meyers and Jef Sutherland

VisualAge for RPG (VARPG) is a rich, full-featured development environment that provides all the tools necessary to build Windows applications for the AS/400. *VisualAge for RPG by Example* brings the RPG language to the GUI world and lets you use your existing knowledge to develop Windows applications. Using a tutorial approach, *VisualAge for RPG by Example* lets you learn as you go and create simple yet functional programs start to finish. The accompanying CD offers a scaled-down version of VARPG and complete source code for the sample project. 236 pages.

We Want Your Response

Mail it ▶

Fax it ▶

Web it ▶

Complete this form to join our network of computer professionals

We'll gladly send you a free copy of

- ❏ *Windows NT Magazine*
- ❏ *NEWS/400*
- ❏ *Selling AS/400 Solutions*
- ❏ *SQL Server Magazine*
- ❏ *Business Finance*

Name _____

Title _____ Phone _____

Company _____

Address _____

City/State/Zip _____

E-mail _____

Where did you purchase this book?

❏ Trade show ❏ Computer store ❏ Internet ❏ Card deck ❏ Bookstore
❏ Magazine ❏ Direct mail catalog or brochure

What new applications do you expect to use during the next year?

_____

_____

How many times this month will you visit a Duke Communications Web site (*29th Street Press, NEWS/400, Selling AS/400 Solutions, SQL Server Magazine, Windows NT Magazine, Business Finance*)? _____

Please share your reaction to *SQL/400 by Example* _____

_____

_____

_____

❏ YES! You have my permission to quote my comments in your publications.
(initials) _____

[99SCXBOOK]

MAKE THE MOST OF YOUR
AS/400 WITH NEWSWIRE/400

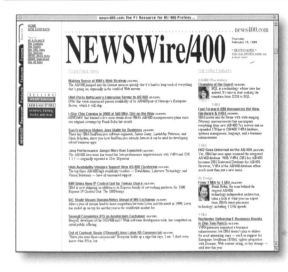

A FREE e-mail newsletter from NEWS/400, the #1 AS/400 magazine worldwide!

Every NEWSWire/400 delivers to your desktop

- Tips & Techniques
- The Latest News from IBM
- Product News
- Industry Updates
- Salary Surveys

Sign up for NEWSWire/400 today & we'll also send you a free sample of NEWS/400, the #1 AS/400 magazine worldwide!

Yes!

☐ I'd like to receive NEWSWire/400 **FREE** via e-mail. Please also send me a sample copy of *NEWS/400* (new subscribers only).

☐ I'd like to receive NEWSWire/400 **FREE** via e-mail. I'd also like to subscribe to *NEWS/400* for $129/year (U.S. only). Please sign me up right away. I understand that I can cancel at any time for a refund.

Copy this page and mail to

**NEWS/400
221 E. 29th St.
Loveland, CO 80538**

**or fax to
(970) 663-4007**

**or subscribe
on the Web at
www.news400store.com**

Name

Title

Company

Address

City/State/Zip

Phone   Fax

E-mail   [99SCDP